Mark Twain in California

THE LITERARY WEST SERIES

SAN FRANCISCO

Mark Twain
in California

The Turbulent California Years of Samuel Clemens

by Nigey Lennon

CHRONICLE BOOKS

THIS BOOK IS DEDICATED
WITH LOVE TO MY HUSBAND, LIONEL ROLFE—
SORT OF A MODERN MARK TWAIN

Copyright © 1982 by Nigey Lennon

Printed in the United States
of America

LIBRARY OF CONGRESS CATALOGING IN
PUBLICATION DATA

Lennon, Nigey, 1954–
Mark Twain in California.
Bibliography: p.122.
1. Twain, Mark, 1835–1910–Homes
and haunts–California. 2. Twain,
Mark, 1835–1910–Careers.
3. Authors, American–19th century–
Biography. 4. Journalists–United
States–Biography. 5. California–
Biography. I. Title.
PS1334.L46 818′.409 [B] 82-4184
ISBN 0-87701-198-2 AACR2

BOOK AND COVER DESIGN
Howard Jacobsen

COMPOSITION
Sara Schrom, Type by Design

EDITING
Harper and Vandenburgh

PHOTO AND ILLUSTRATION CREDITS

Copley Library, La Jolla, California:
pages 10 (bottom left), 28, 112, and 117.

Mark Twain Papers, Bancroft Library,
University of California, Berkeley:
front cover, pages 10 (bottom right), 32,
69, 119, and 120.

Nevada Historical Society: pages 10
(top left and top right), 16, 20, 23, and 24.

The illustrations on the following pages
originally appeared in the first edition
of Twain's *Roughing It*, published in
1870 by American Publishing Co.,
Hartford, Connecticut: pages 27, 46,
58, 61, 70, 72, 74, 103, and 114.

The map on page 15 is by
Nancy Applegate.

CHRONICLE BOOKS
870 Market Street
San Francisco, California 94102

CONTENTS

ACKNOWLEDGMENTS

A book is generally written by one highly visible person, with a crowd of assorted but invisible accomplices massed behind his chair. This book is no different from any other book in that respect, except that I would like to take this opportunity to name my accessories in crime, thus exposing them, along with myself, to the pitiless light of guilt.

The chief culprit in all this must be my husband, Lionel Rolfe, whose brilliant foray into Los Angeles's buried intellectual history, *Literary L.A.*, gave me a great deal of inspiration in my own work. Lionel also served as an admirable guide through the subterranean passages of Los Angeles's main library, and as a model word processor.

The staff of the Mark Twain Papers project at Bancroft Library (University of California, Berkeley) was extremely good-natured and helpful to me during my whirlwind tour of their facilities. Likewise, Robert H. Hirst, present editor of the Mark Twain Papers, was very kind in giving me a copy of his thesis on the influence of Bret Harte on Twain and his writing. John Ahouse, special collections librarian at California State University, Long Beach, supplied me with a steady stream of intelligently chosen data at all stages of my work on this book. Ann Bancroft and Bill Moore, of Oakland, graciously kept me off the streets by allowing me the run of their house during the time I spent in the Bay Area doing research on the book. Toni White lent me her typewriter to patch together the final draft of my manuscript when my own machine went on strike. Thanks to Dick DeRusha's magnificent word-processing equipment in his secret lab in Silver Lake, my grubby typescript was transformed into a fancy manuscript. My father-in-law, Benjamin L. Rolfe, merits my undying gratitude for his constant support during the writing of this book.

And Larry Smith of Chronicle Books deserves a special mention for commissioning this book and thereby enabling me to pay my rent, car payment, and tab at Hollywood Billiards.

Preface

The Reader Who Picks Up

this volume, sees that it is about Mark Twain in California, and then notices that I have no impressive-looking string of academic initials galloping after my name may wonder why I was audacious enough to attempt such an undertaking. Aside from the fact that audacity seems to run in my family, all I can say is that I wanted to enjoy myself while writing, and to me there is no more enjoyable subject than Mark Twain.

In the autumn of 1973, I was living in London and found myself stuck in bed with some unclassifiable malady that any fool but myself would have instantly recognized for the homesickness it was. Having nothing better to do than lie on my lumpy mattress and stare up at the cracks and stains on the ceiling, I finally turned in desperation to a paperback edition of Twain's *The Innocents Abroad* that happened to be propping up the leg of my wobbly nightstand. I had, of course read *Tom Sawyer* and *Huckleberry Finn* as a child, but this was my first heavy duty exposure to the "adult" Twain. I devoured *The Innocents Abroad* in five or six thrilling, hilarious hours, and then I dragged myself up out of my sickbed and headed straight for the nearest public library, where I proceeded to check out every Twain volume they had.

Now, nine years later, I look back and envy myself with all my heart, for I no longer have any major Twain left to read. Over the years I've pretty much read my way through his work until now I'm down to his shopping lists and other scholarly minutiae. Sitting in my dingy flat in London with that enormous armload of Twain books waiting for me to dive into was like being poised, for the first time in my life, on the top of the first steep slope of a gigantic roller coaster. After that one long, exhilarating plummet downwards, everything else has been—well, routine.

That basically sums up how I stumbled into my terminal state of "delirium Clemens." I've been getting worse ever since, thank you. As for the reason why I chose the focus of Twain in California, perhaps because I am a native Californian myself, I feel more at home writing about Twain's Pacific Coast days than about his East Coast ones. I must admit that the history of Twain after he became (in his own words) a "scribbler of books, and an immovable fixture among the other rocks of New England" isn't half as fascinating to me as the time he spent roaming San Francisco's Barbary Coast and the Mother Lode country, rubbing elbows with people from every class of life and gathering vivid and valuable impressions for his future writing. This fascination is increased by the fact that Twain himself tended to downplay his California experiences; thus, in reading the notes he made in his California notebooks, which have only recently been published, or in digging through old newspaper clippings dating back to Twain's California period, it is impossible not to feel at least something of the thrill of discovery. Despite the fact that in California Twain was transformed from a wandering newspaperman into an eloquent and finished author with his own personal voice, few, if any, writers have seen fit to focus on this period of his life. Numerous books exist that cover Twain's life in Nevada, or after he left the Pacific Coast; but none deals solely with Twain in California. It is time, I think, to set the record straight about this fascinating period in the life of Samuel Clemens.

MARK TWAIN IN CALIFORNIA

THIS SERIES OF PHOTOGRAPHS FROM 1861 TO 1868 SHOWS
THE CHANGING FACES OF TWAIN DURING HIS SOJOURN IN THE WEST.

I
PROLOGUE

AT FOUR O'CLOCK ON A
spring morning in 1864, a small group of men huddled in a ravine
about a mile outside of Virginia City, Nevada. The dusty gray light,
speckled with sand, showed that the group had clustered expec-
tantly around two of its number. These two had thrown off their
coats and were rolling up their shirt-sleeves, meanwhile filling the air
with profanity that shook the sagebrush and mesquite to their very
foundations.

The shorter of the two was wiry and belligerent looking, a
sort of human sagebrush himself. He waved his Colt revolver in the
air whenever he had an important point to make; his other form of
punctuation was a rich and varied profanity. His name was Steve
Gillis—an expert marksman, notorious saloon brawler, and, inciden-
tally, a compositor on the Virginia City *Territorial Enterprise*.

The other key member of the group, on whom Gillis was lav-
ishing his prodigious advice, was of medium height, slight, and slope-
shouldered. He had a head of unruly reddish-brown hair, a drooping
moustache, and a look of general disarray about his person. His keen
gray eyes, under bushy brows, marked him as something other than
a laughable derelict, however. His name was Samuel Clemens, and

from his languid drawl one could identify him as a migrant from the Mississippi Valley. Two years previously this unprepossessing wanderer had drifted to Virginia City without a penny in his pocket and had gladly accepted the lowest reporting job on the *Territorial Enterprise*. To the surprise of everyone in Virginia City, he had risen through the ranks during those two years to become the *Enterprise's* star reporter, keeping the public constantly howling over his vitriolic political editorials, fanciful hoaxes, and running commentary on life on the Comstock Lode. As a matter of fact, it was because of his unbridled pen that he happened to be freezing himself to death on this particular morning when he should have been home in bed, sleeping off last night's customary dissipation.

Now, in the chilly desert air, Clemens had just made the rather painful discovery that he was unable to hit a barn door broadside from a distance of five or six feet. The barn door had a fence rail leaning against it, and that fence rail was a symbolic effigy of James. L Laird, the editor of the *Enterprise's* rival paper, the Virginia City *Daily Union*. Clemens had reason to be considerably nervous about his lack of shooting precision, since he had challenged Laird to a duel that was set to begin in an hour, at 5 A.M. If he couldn't hit Laird in effigy, it stood to reason that he wasn't going to be able to hit him in the flesh, either – especially while dodging the volley of bullets that Laird would most likely be firing back at him. At this cheerful thought, Clemens's savage expression grew more savage still, and he leaned over to take another swig from the brown bottle of vile Washoe whiskey at his feet. It wasn't calculated to improve his aim any, but he definitely needed a drink.

Steve Gillis was acting as Clemens's second in the duel – which was only fair, since he and another *Enterprise* staffer, the corpulent and cynical Rollin M. Daggett, had needled Clemens into sending the challenge to Laird in the first place. However, at the moment the compact, peppery Gillis (who was rumored to weigh ninety-five pounds when sodden with "valley tan" and attired in his characteristic tramp printer's garb of frock coat, derby hat, pegged pants, and pointy-toed boots) was thoroughly disgusted with his friend Clemens's marksmanship. In vain did Clemens point out that he had only limited experience with firearms, preferring instead to annihilate those who displeased him from behind the sanctuary of the editorial desk, using verbal ammunition. Gillis stood firm, determined to show Clemens which end of a pistol was up. He snatched Clemens's revolver away from him and blazed away at an unsuspecting sparrow that happened to be flying overhead, and he nearly shot the bird's head off. He pressed the smoking gun back into Clemens's shaking hand and facetiously congratulated him on his "great" shot. "You'll show old Laird a thing or two," he joked. "But don't kill him — just blow his nasty face off."

Laird and his group of supporters came marching staunchly down into the gulley just in time to see this amazing feat of shooting prowess. They had heard the sound of gunfire and had surmised that Clemens and company were getting in some practice. They saw the sparrow's last gasp, but did not arrive in time to ascertain who its murderer was. So Laird demanded who had done the dirty deed, and Steve Gillis promptly gave the credit to Clemens. Laird's second immediately wanted to know how far off the bird had been. "Oh, not far — about thirty yards," replied Gillis blandly.

"How often can Clemens hit his mark?" was the next question.

"Oh, about four times out of five," Gillis lied nonchalantly. At that, Laird gathered his fellows about him and retreated from the field. A little later that day, Clemens received a note from Laird, written in a very shaky hand, declining the honor of fighting any sort of duel whatsoever with the *Enterprise's* star reporter.

The victory celebration over at the *Enterprise* was even more bibulous than usual, or so the story goes.

ACCORDING TO LEGEND,

Samuel Clemens and Steve Gillis were on the Wells Fargo stage to San Francisco within twenty-four hours of the abortive duel. The sending and carrying of challenges had just recently been made a rather serious crime in Nevada by a fiat of Governor James W. Nye — a crime punishable by two years in prison. Since both Clemens and Gillis were well-known figures around Virginia City, it was likely that Nye would feel obliged to make a public example of their shenanigans. Public opinion of Samuel Clemens was sharply divided in Nevada. On the one hand, he often delighted *Enterprise* readers with his ready wit and down-to-earth frontier humor, and he was the toast of the town when it came to the fine art of saloon conversation, or to spinning tall tales beside the barroom stove; but there were those who found Clemens's acidulous political writing to be a less palatable brew, and the more respectable citizens of Virginia City tended to look askance on the fact that this would-be upholder of the public morals sometimes spent the night snoring in the doorways of North C Street, too befuddled to make his way home.

Clemens, however, was no worse in his personal habits than were many inhabitants of Washoe. In a very real sense, he had merely acquired a protective coloration from his surroundings, which were the wide-open world of the gold-rich Comstock. He had arrived in Carson City, the capital of what was then the Nevada Territory, with his brother Orion Clemens, in 1861. As a political favor, Orion had been appointed secretary to James Nye, the territorial governor, through a friend, a member of newly elected President Lincoln's cabinet. Twenty-seven-year-old Sam, having nothing better to do at home, had gone along for the ride. Behind him lay a career as a Mississippi River steamboat pilot—a career that, to his great sorrow, had been cut short by the Civil War, with its embargo on river travel and trade. He had subsequently spent a very brief period—no more than a month—seeing the horrors of that war for himself, as a member of a ragtag Confederate militia unit, before he had decided that war was indeed hell, and had "absquatulated." Discovering that Orion had wangled the appointment as Governor Nye's general factotum, the younger Clemens had decided to accompany his brother on the overland stage trip west from St. Joseph, Missouri, to Carson City.

Samuel Clemens had not originally intended to stay long in the Nevada Territory. Always restless and in need of frequent changes of scenery, he had fixed on the Comstock Lode as an interesting stopping point primarily because of its fabulous gold and silver mines, and his intention had been to get rich quick and then get out. By the mid-1850s, many of the inhabitants of his hometown, Hannibal, Missouri, had snatched up spades and shovels and had hightailed it out of the Midwest, seeking the famous Comstock gold. As a boy, Sam had longed to go with them, but he had laid aside his gold-hungry aspirations to pursue his Mississippi piloting career. Circumstances and his brother Orion's political appointment dovetailed in a most fortuitous way when the Civil War was raging and Sam had been left without an occupation. So he decided to join the great westward expansion in the hope of picking up a bushel or two of the gold nuggets that were rumored to cover the Washoe desert.

When Sam Clemens arrived in Carson City with his brother on the overland stage, the two of them presented a woebegone and unkempt picture to the small crowd lined up at the stage stop to greet them. Perhaps the citizens of Carson had expected to see a pair of tall-hatted dignitaries; instead, they got a couple of scratchy-whiskered roughnecks in sweaty, dust-covered "undress uniform." Whatever they had expected, they were apparently disappointed, for vague plans for a banquet honoring the two new arrivals evaporated almost the moment the Clemenses stepped down from the stagecoach. The welcoming committee mumbled a few words of greeting and then drifted away, leaving the puzzled brothers to hunt up a lodging house and the civilized (for Nevada) pleasure of a chilly bath poured from a tin pail.

Things had not improved appreciably for Samuel Clemens following this inauspicious arrival. Orion's secretaryship, Sam soon discovered, did not include a sinecure for the secretary's brother. The salary Orion received was a mere $1800 a year, at a time when the

SAMUEL CLEMENS, NEWLY ARRIVED IN THE NEVADA
TERRITORY, POSED FOR THIS DANDIFIED PORTRAIT IN THE HOPES OF
IMPRESSING HIS FRIENDS BACK IN HANNIBAL, MISSOURI.

Mark Twain in California

wealth of the Comstock, compounded by the inflation of the Civil War, had driven prices sky-high. A steak dinner in one of Virginia City's better eateries could cost as much as twenty-five dollars, and only the very wealthy could afford to feed and stable horses. As Sam wryly remarked some years later, Orion's meager salary wasn't enough to support his unabridged dictionary—let alone his younger brother.

Not wishing to be beholden to his brother for bed and board, Sam took what little money he could scrape together and traveled around the Territory. The citizens of Carson City had not been overly fond of the young newcomer with his strange habit of leaning against a pole at the intersection of the territorial capital's two main streets; he seemed too lazy for comprehension as he lounged there for hours, puffing on his old pipe and contemplating the humanity that passed him. So he had left Carson to drift from Lake Tahoe (then called Lake Bigler) to the mining town of Unionville in Nevada's Humboldt County, and eventually to Aurora, which lay between California and Nevada, always in search of wealth from mining speculation. He saw his own small savings grow smaller and smaller, and as he pursued unsuccessful mining venture after unsuccessful mining venture, his letters to Orion became desperate: "Send me $50 or $100, all you can spare." The mining fever had him firmly in its grip by the time he had been in the Territory six months. Finally, after being reduced to outright poverty, he had been forced to abandon his mining attempts and take a job at ten dollars a week as a laborer in a quartz mill. It lasted a week, at which time Clemens disgustedly threw up the job and went searching for a legendary "cement mine" reputed to lie near desolate Mono Lake in California, where gold nuggets as thick as raisins in a fruitcake were rumored to be trapped in a vein of cement. He never found the mine; meanwhile his debts continued to pile up.

At that stage of the proceedings, Clemens might very well have been forced to return to Missouri in disgrace, much as he detested the notion, if it hadn't been for a fortuitous circumstance. He had always had a way with words; he had served as an apprentice printer before becoming a Mississippi pilot, and had additionally contributed heavily to the impoverished Hannibal *Journal* during a period when Orion had served as that paper's publisher. He had even been paid for two travel letters he had sent to the *Saturday Post* of

Keokuk, Iowa, at the age of twenty-one. But Clemens did not consider himself a writer, nor did he regard journalism with much respect. He wrote partly to amuse himself and mainly to pick up a couple of dollars here and there.

After arriving in Nevada and seeing enough of it to acquire sufficient impressions, he had written two broad burlesques of territorial life, which he sent to the *Territorial Enterprise* under the pen name "Josh" in the hope of earning enough to keep him in bread and beans for a week or two.

Frontier newspapers at that time were always happy to receive contributions from outside, especially if the pieces happened to be well written; and humor was especially in demand for the hard-pressed and weary frontiersmen. One of Clemens's articles was a portrait of a self-obsessed public lecturer, dubbed "Professor Personal Pronoun." The professor's lecture, according to "Josh," was so egotistical that it couldn't be printed fully – the type cases had been denuded of capital I's before it could be half set. The other article, which caught the sharp eye of the *Enterprise*'s editor, Joseph Goodman, was a satirical Fourth of July oration, which began,"I was sired by the Great American Eagle and foaled by a continental dam."

Clumsy as these attempts at humor were, Goodman saw something in them. He was a rather literate gentleman, and in a couple of years under his direction the *Enterprise*, formerly a rusty frontier weekly, had become a highly successful daily, "printed by steam," with palatial offices and a faithful following. Goodman had accomplished this through a combination of journalistic sagacity and pragmatic understanding of the politics of frontier journalism; in short, he knew very well how to back up his editorial judgment with his revolver when the need arose. With this double-barreled policy, he had earned the respect of the rough-riding inhabitants of Washoe, and the *Enterprise* was not only the best-read sheet in Nevada, but it was eagerly perused by more sophisticated readers in San Francisco and Sacramento as well.

Samuel Clemens's "Josh" contributions struck a chord in Goodman, who recognized some writing talent in this failed prospector. He accordingly instructed his managing editor, one Barstow, to dispatch a letter to Clemens, offering him a job as a local reporter for twenty-five dollars a week. The *Enterprise*'s chief reporter, Dan De Quille (William Wright), was planning at that time on taking a much-needed vacation to visit his wife and family "back in the states," and the paper was in need of another hand at the bellows.

It was late July, 1862, when Clemens received Barstow's letter offering him employment. The letter reached him in the mining camp of Aurora—a part of the country that was either in California or Nevada, depending on which way the wind blew. (It would be considered an unofficial part of California until the state lines were permanently fixed in 1863, at which time the Nevada Territorial Legislature would snatch it away.) When Clemens first read Barstow's letter, he had serious reservations about accepting the job. For one thing, his prospecting fever had not yet broken, even though his budget had. He had recently written to Orion: "I owe about $45 or $50, and have got about $45 in my pocket. But how the hell I am going to live on something over $100 until October or November is singular. The fact is, I must have something to do, and that shortly, too."

Clemens pondered the possibilities awhile longer, taking a walking trip, as he described it to Orion, of "60 or 70 miles through a totally uninhabited country." He did not elaborate further as to his eventual destination, but it is possible that he may have taken one last stab at mining as far away as southern California, where there was considerable prospecting going on in what is now Kern County. He may even have gone as far south as Placerita Canyon, where gold was first discovered in 1842—a spot hardly thirty-five miles outside of what is today Los Angeles. Clemens may have hoped that the southern California mines would deliver him from the ignominy of being a newspaper reporter—a condition he did not relish—but at any rate, if he did make a side trip to southern California, he did not find instant wealth there.

By early August, he had returned to Aurora with his mind more or less made up. It was then that he abandoned the decrepit cabin he had been sharing with his friend Calvin Higbie, and, unable to afford a horse or stagecoach passage, began a 130-mile hike to Virginia City to start his journalistic servitude. The searing August heat of Washoe was a formidable enemy for anyone on foot, so Clemens did his walking by night and spent the days sleeping in haystacks by the side of the narrow track that served as a trail.

When he finally came dragging into the *Enterprise*'s handsome brick building on North C Street in Virginia City, his appearance was truly arresting. He was malodorous with sweat and blanketed

SAMUEL CLEMENS JUST PRIOR TO
THE TIME HE JOINED THE STAFF OF THE VIRGINIA CITY
TERRITORIAL ENTERPRISE.

Mark Twain in California

in alkali dust from the trail; he displayed an almost waist-length, matted red beard; his slouch hat was caved in and disreputable, and went with the rest of his costume; and the evidence of his recent haystack sleeping quarters clung visibly to his clothes. He carried a large bedroll on his back, which he unrolled and threw down the moment he walked into the paper's editorial room, and he wore the ubiquitous Washoe navy revolver on his belt—more for show than for defense, for Clemens was always a miserable marksman.

When this peripatetic apparition hunkered down in front of Joseph Goodman's partner, Denis McCarthy, who was holding down the fort at that particular moment along with Dan De Quille, it spoke in such a long, drawn-out drawl that both McCarthy and De Quille wondered whether it would ever finish its sentence. Clemens reportedly introduced himself thus: "My starboard leg seems to be unshipped. I'd like about one hundred yards of line; I think I am falling to pieces." Then he explained that he had come to take the reporting job which Barstow had offered him. He was accordingly hustled off to bathe and acquire "a more Christian costume," after which he set in to learn his job from the ground up—a subject which he dealt with in *Roughing It* at great length. He remained at the *Enterprise* from August, 1862, through May, 1864.

The Nevada Territory at that time was an excellent place to receive an initiation into the rites of journalism. There are many who claim that the golden era of journalism was the latter half of the nineteenth century, and in the annals of the *Enterprise* there is more than enough evidence to support that claim. Frontier journalism, as exemplified by Goodman's paper, was not the staid, convention-ridden thing that journalism was at that time in other parts of the country. Libel laws were notoriously lax, for one thing, and disagreements were generally settled when the injured party appeared in the *Enterprise* editorial room with his handy six-shooter and demanded an interview with whichever staff member was responsible.

Then, too, personality was a highly desirable and popular quality in Western journalism. The modern reader, used to the antiseptic, "just-the-facts" tone of most present-day newspapers, would probably be rather taken aback by the distinctly nonobjective style evinced by Dan De Quille or Mark Twain in their dissemination of the daily news. The line between fact and fantasy was a nonexistent one on the *Enterprise*, and indeed on many other frontier newspapers of that era. The New England literary nabobs who were later to criticize Clemens's tendency to confuse fantasy and fact must have deliberately discounted the effect of Western journalism on his writing style. Another important point: there was no stigma attached to being a "reporter" rather than a "writer" in those days; in fact, it has been observed that virtually every important Pacific Coast writer at that time had originally written for a newspaper.

In the early 1860s, during Clemens's stay, Virginia City was the archetype of almost all the lawless "wooden" towns that were to follow it in other parts of the West. New gold and silver deposits were forever being discovered, "located," and worked, sometimes with stunning results; there was an endless ebb and flow of colorful characters from all over the country – seduced, as Clemens had been, by the promise of easy riches. As might be imagined, the politics of such a wealthy territory were Byzantine, and the expression "corrupt politician" was almost a redundancy. In covering the Nevada Territorial Legislature, Clemens learned enough about politics to last him a lifetime. (He would later learn even more about political corruption in San Francisco.)

When all else failed, there was always a rival newspaper to abuse and revile – one which would abuse and revile you in turn. This pastime of exchanging journalistic compliments would ultimately prove to be Clemens's undoing; but it was primarily looked upon as good fun, even when somebody wound up getting winged in the process of taking potshots at a journalistic rival.

But the single most important feature of Clemens's sojourn on the *Enterprise*, at least as far as literary history was concerned, was the fact that he had become Mark Twain while working there. In those days, nearly all Western journalists wrote under catchy pseudonyms. Dan De Quille, as we have seen, was William Wright to his wife back in the Midwest, although all his Washoe comrades thought of him as nothing but Dan. Samuel Clemens had accordingly tried on and subsequently discarded a few pseudonymic inventions of his own, starting with "Josh," before he finally settled on the one that was eventually to emblazon itself so brilliantly across the annals of American literature. (One wonders what Clemens would have thought if he had known that his new moniker would one day blaze forth from such articles of commerce as boxes of cigars, or that he would eventually have to have it copyrighted out of necessity.)

A GROUP OF NEVADA TERRITORY JOURNALISTS.
MARK TWAIN IS THE SECOND FIGURE FROM THE LEFT WITH HIS
ARM ON HIS NEIGHBOR'S SHOULDER; JOSEPH GOODMAN,
PUBLISHER OF THE VIRGINIA CITY *TERRITORIAL ENTERPRISE*, HAS THE
NUMBER "2" DIRECTLY ABOVE HIS HEAD; STEVE GILLIS
IS THIRD FROM THE RIGHT IN THE BOTTOM ROW.

The origin of the name "Mark Twain" had its beginnings during Clemens's Mississippi piloting days in the 1850s. There had been a rather vainglorious and bombastic old fellow, a steamboat pilot himself, who had contributed wordy diatribes to the New Orleans *Picayune*, and who was known to all the pilots on the river, including Clemens. The articles written by this personage were full of largely spurious river navigation information and sentimental gush about the river's "good old days," and they irritated Clemens no end. The author of these compositions was named Isaiah Sellers, but he used the *nom de plume* "Mark Twain" – "mark twain" in river jargon signifying two fathoms, or twelve feet, of water, the shallowest depth a steamboat could enter without fear of running aground.

Clemens had gotten so fed up with Sellers's self-important carryings-on that he had taken matters into his own hands. One day the *Picayune* carried a clumsy but blunt burlesque of Sellers's windy style, signed "Sergeant Fathom." When the original "Mark Twain"

Twain in Virginia City in 1864 with
fellow Washoe journalists A.J. Simmons (left)
and Billy Clagget.

read this satire, it took the steam right out of his boilers. Sellers was so hurt and humiliated, in fact, that he vowed he would never write another line. Apparently, he didn't; Clemens had accomplished his aim.

In Nevada in 1863, Clemens received word that Sellers had died, and he waxed somewhat remorseful. He decided that "Mark Twain" would be an excellent pen name to assume, partly because it painted intriguing images of his colorful past on the Mississippi, but also because it served as a tip of the hat to the departed Sellers. Clemens, with an ever-sharp eye, also knew that Sellers, since he was no longer in the land of the living, would hardly be able to sue him for misappropriating his name. So was Mark Twain born.

IRONICALLY ENOUGH, MARK

Twain had much of Virginia City in the palm of his hand when, in May, 1864, the fiasco occurred that cost him his job and sent him fleeing to California. By this time, he rarely had to write mundane or routine news stories, but could indulge in whatever extravagant satire he had a burning urge to write. Those satires were making a name for him on both sides of the Sierra Nevada, for some of his *Enterprise* articles were beginning to be reprinted in San Francisco and Sacramento papers. Still, Virginia City had lost much of its original novelty for Twain. After all, colorful characters were a dime a dozen, stabbings and shootings were so routine that they didn't even rate a paragraph on the paper's back page, and you could take part in just so many carousals in the town's saloons before you felt like throwing in the towel. This is how Twain described his restlessness in *Roughing It*: "I wanted to see San Francisco. I wanted to go somewhere. I wanted—and I did not know what I wanted. I had the 'spring fever' and wanted a change, principally, no doubt."

Twain's spring fever ultimately embroiled him in a complex situation involving prominent citizens in Virginia City and Carson City, as well as James Laird, editor of the *Enterprise*'s rival paper, the Virginia City *Daily Union*. The debacle, which forever after was known as "The Great Sanitary Fund Fiasco," was almost a textbook example of Western journalism, with its fiery feuds between competing newspapers and its P.T. Barnum–like circulation wars in which each rival attempted to outdo the other with wilder and more improbable stunts—some of them taking place in the flesh, but the bulk of them dreamed up "for show" and played out only on the pages of the paper in question. For a number of years, for instance, the *Enterprise* had never lost an opportunity to heap opprobrium upon the Wabuska *Mangler*, a mangy little sheet published, or rumored to be published, in the mining town of Wabuska. Wabuska was far enough away from Virginia City to keep the ostensibly out-raged *Mangler* staff from descending on the *Enterprise* editorial rooms en masse and wreaking a terrible vengeance. At the time of the *Enterprise's* attack on the *Mangler*, it should be noted, the town of Wabuska boasted five or six shacks, a saloon, a general store—and no newspaper whatsoever, but that didn't stop the *Enterprise*. On such an imaginative foundation had the *Enterprise* built its reputation.

What a reporter thought of as humor was, of course, some-times looked upon in quite a different light by the reading public. Thus, when Mark Twain, in the throes of spring fever (or perhaps recovering from a mammoth hangover), decided to stick his journal-istic harpoon into the side of the Sanitary Fund, many readers of the *Enterprise* were not amused.

The Sanitary Fund was the Civil War equivalent of today's Red Cross. In 1864, some bright and enterprising soul had come up with the idea of auctioning off a symbolic sack of flour in various Western communities, with the auction proceeds all going into the coffers of the Sanitary Fund—presumably to render medical aid to both Union and Confederate wounded. Nevada was a hotbed of warring factions at the time of the Sanitary flour sack drive; and though there were both Unionists and Confederate sympathizers in the Territory, the Confederates were in the majority in Carson City and Virginia City. About May 16, 1864, the Sanitary Fund flour sack reached Gold Hill, a suburb of Virginia City. In the parade her-alding the celebrated sack's triumphal entrance into Gold Hill marched none other than Mark Twain, accompanied by several other *Enterprise* staffers. The Gold Hill *Evening News* rather snidely observed that "tone was given to the procession by the presence of Gov. Twain and his staff of bibulous reporters, who came in a free carriage, ostensibly for the purpose of taking notes, but in reality in pursuit of free whiskey."

Maybe Twain was more bibulous than usual, or it may have been that he was still rather uncomfortable with the whole issue of the Civil War and its gallant boys in uniform. Not only had his own

THE GREAT FLOUR SACK PROCESSION.

war career been—well, irregular, but, like many other natives of border states such as Missouri, he suffered from sharply divided sensibilities on the entire slavery question. His family had owned slaves, but had been antislavery. Clemens's sojourn in Nevada had eventually turned him into a Union sympathizer and a half-hearted abolitionist, and he looked on his experience in a homespun Confederate militia unit with some embarrassment. In later years, of course, he would write *Huckleberry Finn*, the greatest abolitionist novel of them all.

Whatever the reason, the day after the flour sack arrived in Virginia City, Twain sat down and wrote an article entitled, "How Is It?" The article suggested that the good Southern-sympathizing ladies of Carson City, who had put on a fancy dress ball to raise money for the Sanitary Fund, had actually elected to ship the proceeds of that ball to "a Miscegenation Society somewhere in the East." At least, it hinted darkly, the ladies were intending to divert the funds *somewhere* dishonorable.

Twain later admitted in a letter to his sister-in-law, Mollie Clemens (Orion's wife), that he had been drinking when he wrote this attack, and that it had never been intended for print, but that the wretched thing had somehow found its way into the *Enterprise*'s

TWAIN IN 1864 WHEN HE WAS SCANDALIZING WASHOE
AS "CITY EDITOR" OF THE VIRGINIA CITY *TERRITORIAL ENTERPRISE*.

composing room and had then burst forth to horrify the Confederate society dames of Carson.

Four of the ladies promptly fired off a damning epistle to the *Enterprise*, which did what every red-blooded Western journal was supposed to do under the circumstances; it stood behind its reporter. The *Enterprise* did not print the ladies' letter, and it also refused to run a retraction of the offending article. The ladies' complaint finally appeared in the *Enterprise*'s rival paper, the *Daily Union*, about a week later. The *Union* saw its chance to really wallop the *Enterprise*, and it furthered the fray by publishing a couple of articles in rapid succession, pointing out that the scurrilous Twain had been accusing its employees of boasting that they had raised a "certain amount of money for the Sanitary Fund, but had never quite gotten around to paying it into the Fund's coffers."

Then the *Union* went one step further. Its proprietor, James Laird, and one of its printers, J.W. Wilmington, responded in print to these accusations of Twain's—although unfortunately they couldn't name him outright, since the original "How Is It?" article had been unsigned. Still, the author was known to everyone—there was no mistaking the tone of that original editorial.

There followed an exchange of nasty correspondence among Laird, Wilmington, and Steve Gillis—a formalized "c'mon out and fight, you big bully" that was quite popular in Nevada in such situations. The *Enterprise* was only too happy to publish all this correspondence in full, of course, because it not only entertained and titillated the readers, but kept the whole situation at the boiling point. To make things even more interesting and complicated, Twain attempted to apologize to the wronged ladies of Carson City in another editorial, the title of which was "Miscegenation." That title alone would seem to indicate that his apology was not as humble and contrite as one might have wished it to be.

Finally Laird agreed to settle the matter on the field of honor, with the results described earlier. At first Twain had been understandably reluctant; but Gillis and Rollin Daggett had laid siege to him, and at last he had capitulated. Then came the early-morning scene in the ravine; and within twenty-four hours of the "duel," Twain and Steve Gillis were on the stage to San Francisco. Behind drawn blinds, they tore out of Virginia City and headed over the Divide for San Francisco, where Twain was subsequently to stumble into his rendezvous with literary destiny. His Washoe days had given him a useful trade; in California, he would, albeit gropingly and haltingly, begin to make something of himself at last.

2
CLEMENS GETS THE "CALL"

AS MARK TWAIN GALLOPED

across the Sierra toward his new life, the *Enterprise* was mourning its loss—after a fashion. "Mark Twain," observed the paper in a tongue-in-cheek editorial only slightly tainted by sentimentality, "has abdicated the local column of the *Enterprise*, where by the grace of Cheek, he so long reigned Monarch of Mining Items, Detailer of Events, Prince of Platitudes, Chief of Biographers, Expounder of Unwritten Law, Puffer of Wildcat, Profaner of Divinity, Detractor of Merit, Flatterer of Power, Recorder of Stage Arrivals, Pack Trains, Hay Wagons, and Things in General." This obituary went on to observe that Twain would "not be likely to shock the sensibilities of San Francisco long. The ordinances against nuisances are stringently enforced in that city."

San Francisco was not unfamiliar with Twain at the time he took up residence there—nor was he unfamiliar with it. He had made the journey over the mountains from Washoe to the Golden Gate on two or three prior occasions, and had sent back articles to the *Enterprise* describing his impressions of the bustling metropolis that was both a suburb of the Comstock Lode and the final destination for the Washoe speculator who struck it rich. Nevada looked to San Francisco for leadership in matters of culture and civilization, while San Francisco welcomed the Washoe mining nabobs with open arms, since it was largely with Comstock wealth that the city by the bay had built up its glittering testimonial to the good life.

Mark Twain had been very impressed by what he had seen on his visits to San Francisco. In one letter, written to his mother, Jane Clemens, and his sister, Pamela Moffett, back in Hannibal, Missouri, he had described some of the the pleasures of life in the teeming city, and had added the plaintive comment, "How I do hate to go back to Washoe!" He would further delineate the pleasures of San Francisco in an article written for the *Enterprise* about a month after he moved to San Francisco, and which was reprinted in the San Francisco *Golden Era*. "To a Christian who has toiled months and months in Washoe," he wrote, "whose hair bristles from a bed of sand, and whose soul is caked with the cement of alkali dust; whose nostrils know of no perfume but the rank odor of the sage-brush— and whose eyes know no landscape but the barren mountains and desolate plains; where the winds blow, and the sun blisters, and the broken spirit of the contrite heart finds joy and peace only in Limberger cheese and lager beer—unto such a Christian, verily the Occidental Hotel (in San Francisco) is Heaven on the half shell. He may even secretly consider it to be heaven on the entire shell, but his religion teaches a sound Washoe Christian that it would be sacrilege to say it." In Twain's opinion, "the birds, and the flowers, and the Chinamen, and the winds, and the sunshine, and all the things that go to make life happy, are present in San Francisco to-day, just as they are all days in the year."

When Twain arrived in San Francisco that May of 1864, he had with him a large trunk half full of miscellaneous mining stock he had acquired in Washoe. His first crude attempts at striking it rich by plying pick and shovel in mining claims had matured during his *Enterprise* days into a more sophisticated modus operandi of speculating in mining stocks. Part of the reason he was glad to leave the Nevada Territory and go to San Francisco was because it appeared that at any moment, the Nevada Territory would become a full-blown state. This change in government, it was generally believed, would have a pronounced effect on the mining stock market and its regulation. Twain reasoned that the stocks he held, especially some valuable Hale and Norcross shares, would appreciate considerably

Bradley & Rulofson, S. F., Cal.
PATENT APPLIED FOR

A PORTRAIT OF TWAIN TAKEN IN SAN FRANCISCO
FOR USE ON HIS VISITING CARD.

Mark Twain in California

before the bottom finally dropped out, as it was likely to do. He intended to sell them when their value was the highest and then live a millionaire's life in a Nob Hill mansion. Either that, or he would take a trip to New York, after which he would return to his family in Missouri – the glorious return of the prodigal son. This entire process, he rather naively believed, would take a month at the longest.

The last thing Twain wanted to do was continue his servitude as a journalistic wage slave. He had enjoyed his *Enterprise* days, but it was his intention to enrich himself with Comstock wealth and become a gentleman of leisure, not continue as a toiling minion in some dingy editorial office. Nonetheless, his Hale and Norcross stock, unsold, was not going to pay his board bill while he awaited just the right moment to sell it. Thus after spending the best part of two weeks in "butterfly idleness," as he phrased it, staying at the opulent Occidental Hotel and sallying forth, dressed to the teeth, to the town's gilded palaces of amusement (he even attended the opera, or so he claimed in *Roughing It*), Twain found himself obliged to take a reporter's job on the San Francisco *Morning Call*. At the same time, Steve Gillis also went to work for the *Call* as a compositor.

Twain's writing was fairly well known in San Francisco, and the *Call* had previously published some of Twain's articles about the "flush times" of Nevada mining. He was no stranger to the paper's publisher, so when he appeared in the *Call*'s Commercial Street offices and asked the paper's owner and chief editor, George Barnes, to take him on as a reporter "just until I can make a stake," Barnes did not turn him away. At first Barnes gave Twain a few desultory assignments, as well as lending the impecunious future millionaire five dollars. Not too long afterward, Clemens was made the *Call*'s "city editor" – a position considerably beneath the one he had left behind him in Virginia City, it might be noted.

He was what was known in journalistic lingo rather pejoratively as a "lokulitems" – meaning that he was responsible for gathering all of the local news and writing it up for publication. This included everything from police court matters to coverage of plays and concerts, with just about anything in between. When news was hard to come by, he and his occasional fellow staffers gathered "such material as we might, wherewith to fill our required columns – and if there were no fires to report we started some." Twain's duties on the *Call* corresponded to those of a present-day general assignment reporter in the sense that he had to be able to write about any-thing. Big metropolitan newspapers still have general assignment re-porters, but they also have reporters who cover "beats." The latter cover their regular news beats—police, courts, city hall, or whatever—but call their stories in to a rewrite man in the city room. On the *Call*, Clemens was general assignment reporter, beat reporter, and rewrite man, all compressed into one grueling but underpaid job—for during most of the four months he spent working on the *Call*, he was most likely the only full-time reporter and rewrite man the paper employed. He was later to explain with thinly disguised irritation that George Barnes figured there was enough work for one and a half reporters, but not two. For this heroic amount of work, Clemens was paid forty dollars a week, although when he wrote about his *Call* experiences in later years, he reduced his salary to fifteen dol-lars for histrionic purposes.

Twain recalled in his *Autobiography* many years later that dur-ing his days on the *Call* he made the rounds of his various news beats from eight or nine in the morning until eleven at night, at which time he sat down in the office to convert his notes into news stories. "It was awful drudgery for a lazy man, and I was born lazy," he admit-ted. Most workdays ended around 2 A.M. It was little wonder, then, that he began to pine for the old freewheeling *Enterprise* days when news was often gathered over lingering champagne lunches at Chauvin's Restaurant and an acceptable news story was anything his fertile imagination could conjure up.

The *Call*, it must be admitted, frowned on reportorial ex-cess—it preferred a steady diet of news items about, as Twain put it, "the squabbles of the night before . . . usually between Irishmen and Irishmen, and Chinamen and Chinamen, with now and then a squabble between the two races for a change." This policy sprung from the fact that the *Call* prided itself on being "the washerwoman's paper," the daily with the biggest circulation in San Francisco. In 1864, when Clemens assumed his reportorial duties there, the paper had already been in existence for eight years. Despite its circulation, it was a second-rate operation (why else would it hire only one full-time reporter?), unable until 1869 to join the telegraphic combine cornered by more successful San Francisco journals such as the *Alta California* and the *Bulletin*, even though telegraph lines had been in since 1861. With such poor links to national news developments, the

Call was obliged to make a virtue of a necessity by placing more emphasis on local news—or its reporter's ingenuity in gathering same. For this reason alone, Twain's job as the *Call's* "lokulitems" would probably have been more than any one reporter could have handled—let alone a reporter with Twain's idiosyncratic work habits. During his *Enterprise* days, Clemens had developed a tendency to leave his information-gathering unaccomplished until the last possible minute, and then to attempt to fill in any factual gaps with flashy writing in order to meet his deadline.

This tendency became ever more pronounced during the four months Twain toiled in the *Call's* depressing offices. As the work grew less interesting and more wearing, he became correspondingly more sluggish and disinterested. His chief complaint, besides the fact that the hours were long, was that he was allowed almost no latitude in his writing. "Just the facts" was all that the *Call* was interested in, and if it hadn't occurred to him before, Twain soon came to realize that he was extremely ill-suited to such a regime.

Clemens's opinions were unwelcome in the *Call's* news columns because they were presumed to be unpopular with the paper's readership. George Barnes considered his average reader to be a lower-middle-class Irish washerwoman, and the paper unabashedly pandered to her tastes in reading matter by slanting all material along very mundane lines. A subscription to the *Call* cost twelve and a half cents per week, making it the cheapest daily available in San Francisco at the time. It soon became Clemens's belief that the *Call's* cheapness was not limited solely to its subscription price, but he had the wisdom to keep such treasonous thoughts to himself, at least while he was working there.

Although Twain had some serious reservations about the nature of his duties at the *Call*, he had a fairly good relationship with George Barnes. He seems to have respected Barnes as a human being if not as an editor. For his part, Barnes was fond of Twain and saw real, if undisciplined, talent in him, but privately he doubted that his languid, red-haired employee was really cut out for a reporter's grueling schedule. In his memoirs, Barnes recalled that Twain fell far short of fulfilling his obligations as itemizer of local news because he was so intolerably slow in getting around his news beat, and even slower when it came to writing up the information. It was painfully clear to Barnes that sooner or later Clemens would reach the end of his rope by himself, and it is a testimony to Barnes's diplomacy that Twain remained reasonably friendly with him when the smoke cleared.

For things, as they often seemed to do with Twain, were once again about to blow sky-high. Just as his innate restlessness had been suddenly brought into sharp focus by the Sanitary Fund fiasco back in Nevada, so matters at the *Call* took a severe turn for the worse when Twain banged his head against the paper's inflexible policy of journalistic redlining.

One day, while making his rounds in search of news, Twain observed a Chinese laundryman being abused, stoned, and derided by a group of young white bullies while a local constable merely stood by and observed the cruel proceedings without lifting a finger. When Twain witnessed this brutal tableau, his torpor and lassitude instantly melted away, and he dashed back to the *Call*, where he wrote up the incident with far more passion than he had felt about any story since going to work there. He submitted his article, in which he castigated the city of San Francisco for the racism of its police force, and went home satisfied that he had done a good turn for the oppressed Asian population. The next day, he looked through the paper with great eagerness, expecting to find his blast at Pacific Coast racism in one of the columns. To his disappointment, the article was nowhere to be seen.

Twain promptly went up to the composing room, where he found the article in question "tucked away among condemned matter on the standing galley." One of the printers told him that Barnes had been responsible for the banishment of the article, so Twain marched straight into his boss's office and demanded an explanation.

The eternally unflappable Barnes patiently reminded his fiery-tempered reporter about the *Call's* staunch supporters, the Irish working class. These people did not look kindly upon the new wave of Chinese immigrant labor that was sweeping into San Francisco, working for next to nothing and threatening to knock the Irish out of the labor market. If the *Call* suddenly took to publishing a bunch of sentimental hogwash defending these coolies, said Barnes, then the paper's subscribers would most assuredly take their reading custom elsewhere.

Twain recognized that his boss's explanation was the very soul of reason—or what at least passed for reason in those parts—but the original issue had not been resolved to his satisfaction. The entire incident marked the beginning of the end for him at the *Call,* and both he and Barnes knew it.

Meanwhile the domestic

life of Twain and Steve Gillis was every bit as colorful as Twain's *Call* duties were ennervating. During their four-month tenure on the *Call,* the two roommates (for they were roommates, since neither was an acceptable roommate to anyone else) switched their lodgings five times, partly to escape such irritations as yapping dogs and tinkling pianos in adjacent apartments, but mostly for amusement. Their restlessness was at least somewhat connected with the grueling monotony of their respective jobs, and both reminisced often about their wild days in Virginia City, swearing to one another that they would go back one day when their financial picture had improved.

Despite all its annoyances, however, Twain realized that his reporter's job had its good points. "No other occupation," he was later to write of his *Call* days, "brings man into such familiar sociable relations with all grades and classes of people. . . . Why, I breakfasted almost every morning with the Governor, dined with the principal clergyman, and slept in the station house."

Twain's familiarity, and his fascination, with the police courts of San Francisco were considerable. He spent a good part of each workday prowling the station house and ascertaining what cases were on the docket for the police court. The main jail, an institution horrible in the exquisitely dreary red-brick manner of nineteenth-century houses of incarceration, was almost always full of prisoners with interesting stories. After being on the job for a while, Twain realized that there was a regular cast of characters in the lockup— indigents, drunks, prostitutes, and other members of the lowest classes of society. The prostitutes and "lost women" in the city jail especially seemed to intrigue Twain, and he wrote many an item in the *Call* detailing their perpetual cycle of life between the streets and the jail. Many of these women, he noted, had once been respectable citizens with husbands and children; perhaps they had begun to drink and had lost their husbands, or their husbands had left them for some other reason, and this abandonment, because the women were powerless to earn a living, often precipitated a dependency on alcohol. In Nevada, Twain had seen very few women of any class, and thus it was extremely educational for him to come face-to-face with women who were neither intrinsically good nor intrinsically bad, but merely the victims of the morality of a fundamentally lawless society covered with a thin veneer of gentility.

In dealing with the police on a daily basis, Twain grew to loathe them for their corruption and smugness. The only really scathing article of his to appear in the *Call* was about corruption and gross incompetence in the police force, a fiery attack that ran under the headline, "What Have the Police Been Doing?" It vividly described the brutality in the city jail, and pointed out that the political machinery that controlled the selection of candidates for the police force was largely to blame. Needless to say, this article did not stand him in good stead with the local constabulary. Martin G. Burke, San Francisco's chief of police, took especial note of the muckraking reporter, and eventually Twain was to find that San Francisco was too hot to hold him and his sense of outrage.

He didn't always resort to inflammatory writing when it came to expressing his disgust with the police, however. One afternoon he was wandering around looking for grist for the news mill when he spotted a large, burly policeman fast asleep on his beat. Twain immediately rushed over to a nearby greengrocer's stand and grabbed the biggest cabbage leaf he could find. Then he proceeded back to the corner where the sleeping policeman was peacefully snoring, and commenced fanning him with it. He abandoned his post only when a large crowd had gathered around, nudging one another and smirking. The next day the story was all over town that Mark Twain had caught one of San Francisco's finest asleep on the job. For its part, the police force chalked up another strike against Twain, and the situation worsened infinitely.

Journalism wars were as prevalent among the San Francisco newspapers as they had been in Nevada, and were riddled with an equal if not a greater amount of skulduggery. One of Twain's journalistic rivals, beginning when he was reporting for the *Call* and continuing during the time he lived in San Francisco, was Albert S. Evans. Evans, at first the San Francisco correspondent for the Gold Hill *Evening News* of Washoe, later became city editor of the San Francisco *Alta California* — defender of the police force, bootlicker of corrupt politicians, and firm supporter of the status quo. Evans wrote for the *Evening News* under the pseudonym "Amigo," and for the *Alta* as "Fitz Smythe." The two reporters, it should be pointed out, were writing for competing publications. At first when Twain wrote about Fitz Smythe he merely poked fun at him in a general way. One of his early editorials, for instance, described Evans's horse, an overworked creature whom Fitz Smythe was, according to Twain, too cheap to feed properly. The animal's diet, said Twain, consisted primarily of old newspapers that the *Alta* received in exchange for copies of its own journal.

The rivalry between Clemens and Evans eventually worsened, and Fitz Smythe began hurling all sorts of unsavory accusations at Twain in print, calling him a "sage-brush Bohemian" and continually imprecating him for lust, drunkenness, and general instability. Twain, although he responded heatedly to these attacks, did not draw similar attention to Evans's private life. Although it was the nature of Pacific Coast journalists to take cheap shots and low blows when attacking an opponent, it is true that Twain was rather outside the pale of polite San Francisco society during this period of his life, just as it was true that Evans's politics were hopelessly reactionary when viewed alongside Twain's. Evans's ethics, however, were considerably less than Clemens's, and his vitriolic spite in the *Alta* and *Evening News* was pronounced even in that era of scurrilous journalistic practice.

By midsummer, mining

stock had soared sky-high, and Clemens was trembling on the edge of his seat as he waited for prices to rise just high enough so he could sell his Hale and Norcross stock. But he waited too long, and suddenly the bottom dropped right out of the stock market. Overnight, Twain's treasured Hale and Norcross had become worth less than the fancy parchment it was printed on. As Twain recalled it, "The wreck was complete. The bubble scarcely left a microscopic moisture behind it. I was an early beggar, and a thorough one."

His sudden plummet downward to despair was part of what Twain would one day describe as "the queer vicissitudes of life on the Pacific Coast." Heartsickness assailed the would-be millionaire as he surveyed his suddenly unbearable situation. He was so distressed at losing all hope of ever becoming a millionaire that he did the unthinkable—he stayed away from his desk at the *Call* for a day after the disaster, which worked a mighty hardship on the paper. He returned to work the following day, resolving "to put up with my thirty-five dollars a week" (actually it was forty) "and forget all about it."

But the torpor and lassitude that he had been successfully fighting off until now suddenly began to wash over him like a huge, greasy wave. He found his work so wearing that George Barnes began keeping an increasingly watchful eye on his failing lokulitems, and was seen to shake his head more and more over Clemens's sketchy copy. Even the advent of a large earthquake that October failed to arouse Twain's interest. He managed to get out a series of reports in which he focused on the human-interest angle of the earthquake, but although the articles were humorous enough, it was plain that Twain's heart wasn't in his work. The earthquake was big news all over the Pacific Coast, and Twain also sent reports of it back to the *Enterprise*. C.C. Goodwin, who served as the *Enterprise's* publisher after Joe Goodman gave up newspaper publishing and went off to consummate a lifelong obsession with archaeology, recalled one of the earthquake dispatches Twain sent to Nevada from California. It contained one paragraph that read:

When that earthquake came on Sunday morning last there was but one man in San Francisco that showed any presence of mind, and he was over in Oakland. He did just what I thought of doing, what I would have done had I had any opportunity—he went down out of his pulpit and embraced a woman. The newspapers said it was his wife. Maybe it was, but if it was it was a pity. It would have shown so much more presence of mind to have embraced some other gentleman's wife.

This clergyman may have been the same one who, according to Twain, was preaching to his flock when the temblor struck. At the first shock, the man of God admonished his congregation, "Keep your seats! There is no better place to die than this!" After the third shock, however, he added, "But outside is good enough!"—and he skipped out the back door.

IT WAS ONLY A MATTER OF

time before Smiggy McGlural made his fateful entrance, ending Twain's stint at the *Call*. Toward the end of his four months as lokulitems, Twain asked Barnes if his workload might not be cut back some, along with his pay, which he agreed could be reduced from forty to twenty-five dollars a week. While he complained to Barnes about the long hours, Twain kept the real truth to himself – he wanted to quit the *Call*, but he couldn't afford to. His disenchantment with the paper had begun with the Chinese persecution incident, and had become almost unendurable by the time the collapsed stock market beggared him. With characteristic honesty, he considered his days at the *Call* numbered, and in idle moments he wondered just how the axe was going to fall.

The innocent-appearing hatchet man in Twain's *Call* demise turned out to be the aforementioned Smiggy McGlural. At the time Clemens had complained that there was just too much work for him to handle alone, Barnes had suggested that he find himself an assistant. Downstairs in the newspaper's counting room there was a young fellow, "a great hulking creature" according to Twain. His name was William McGrew, but an irreverent copyboy had dubbed him Smiggy McGlural and the name had stuck because it seemed appropriate somehow. With a little fast talking – a feat of which he was supremely capable – Twain was able to persuade McGlural that a reporter's life was endlessly entertaining, and that it was just the thing for him. Twain was so convincing, in fact, that he soon had the bumbling McGlural handling most of the work that he himself was supposed to be doing. McGlural, needless to say, had no journalistic background and even less intellectual capacity, but as Twain remarked in his *Autobiography*, "Mentality was not required or needed in a *Morning Call* reporter and so he conducted his office to perfection."

McGlural resembled many another starry-eyed journalistic apprentice in that he had an abundance of energy but no corresponding writing talent. As Twain played an ever-smaller role in the *Call*'s writing department, Smiggy's peculiar style of journalism became ever more apparent – sometimes perhaps too much so. Smiggy's idea of a breezy description of a costume ball, for instance, was an unintentional parody of the flowery style of the day. "Terpsichore and Apollo met at the Pavilion last night with their host of retainers," gushed McGlural in genuine gee-whiz style. "Orpheus was there with them; and with music and with dancing the hours wore away, until the time of night was represented by the small figures. . . . Apollo, and old Charon himself, were industriously doing the agree-

able. The affair passed off finely. There was no lack of enjoyment."
Especially for Twain.

George Barnes, however, was less than tickled. He sternly re-
quested Clemens's presence in his office. When the guilty party
shuffled in, scraping one foot after the other as he was wont to do
when he was about to be raked over the coals, Barnes fixed him with
a knowing scowl and asked him point-blank, "Do you know what I
think of you as a local reporter?"

Twain had to answer in the negative. He had some idea, it
was true, but he didn't want to hang himself prematurely.

"You're out of your element, Clemens. This position requires
persistence and a certain attention to detail. I believe you are un-
suited to it. Besides, you're obviously capable of greater things in
literature."

"Oh, I see. You mean to say that I don't suit you," replied
Twain with mock diffidence.

"Yes, to be truthful, that's exactly what I mean," admitted
Barnes.

Twain was glad to offer his resignation, even though it meant
he no longer had a twenty-five-dollar-a-week salary to squander on
such frivolities as food and lodging. But he had to admit to himself
that Barnes had been pretty slow; after all, he himself had known
the minute he went to work for the *Call* that he was totally unfit for
the duties of a lokulitems.

In 1906, when mark twain

was finishing out his life as a nationally acclaimed man of letters on
the East Coast, he had reason to remember his dismissal from the
Morning Call. It was in April of that year that the famous San Francisco earthquake and fire drew immediate attention to the city, with
overwrought descriptions screaming forth from the pages of every
newspaper, along with dramatic photos of the wreckage and ruin left
behind.

By chance, one of the first photographs Twain saw happened
to show the remains of the original *Call* building, with the magnificent structure's ruined walls crumbling around its charred and black-
ened foundation. (The *Call*, like Clemens, had prospered in the in-
tervening years, and had taken up far more palatial quarters as a result of its prosperity.)

Twain was in the process of dictating notes for his *Autobiography* at the time of the earthquake, and as a result of seeing that picture of the ruined former *Call* building he was moved to point out that even though Providence had been a little late in wreaking vengeance on the *Call* for firing him some forty years earlier, that vengeance had finally arrived. When Providence had decided to attend to business at last, said Twain, it had done an admirable job of it. He observed that it did seem a little extreme, perhaps, that Providence had chosen to lay waste to most of San Francisco in order to demolish the old *Call* building, but to back up the judgment of the heavenly retribution committee he cited the case of a man who went home swearing from a prayer meeting; nine months later, that man's wife and seven children all died long, agonizing deaths. It didn't really seem fair, Twain had to admit, but the ways of Providence were often difficult to fathom. Providence had intended to punish the man for his blasphemy, and if the man had any intelligence, he probably realized that the intention had been carried out, although mainly at the expense of other people. But, Twain reasoned, he had known all along that sooner or later Providence would even up the score with the *Call*—after all, he had been raised a Presbyterian, with an unshakable faith in the power of good over evil.

3
THE SAGEBRUSH
BOHEMIAN

AFTER LOSING HIS POSITION
on the *Call*, Twain entered into a period of greater or lesser impecu-
niosity. With his weekly paycheck gone, he was obliged for a while
to depend on the sporadic income he received from contributing to
San Francisco literary journals such as the *Golden Era*, some of
which he had written for during his Washoe days. The *Era*
sometimes paid its contributors as much as five dollars for an
especially long article—a rate that varied not one bit even if the
contributor happened to be as well known on the Pacific Coast as
was "the Washoe Giant."

As a result of his sparse and infrequent income, Twain recalled, he became "very adept at slinking. I slunk from back street to
back street, I slunk away from approaching faces that looked familiar,
I slunk to my meals, ate them humbly and with mute apology for
every mouthful I robbed my generous landlady of, and at midnight,
after wanderings that were but slinkings away from cheerfulness
and light, I slunk to my bed." When he wasn't slinking away from his
financial responsibilities, Twain slunk up to the bar rail at the
numerous saloons where he was a regular enough customer to have
a running tab. As a reporter for the *Call*, as well as on his previous

visits to San Francisco, he had spent considerable time in the city's drinking establishments, and more than one of his fellow elbow-benders was to observe that the name "Mark Twain" had less to do with life on the Mississippi than it had to do with Clemens's custom of marking up a couple of shots on credit.

However, Twain did not have to suffer the dark side of "the queer vicissitudes of life on the Pacific Coast" for very long. Shortly after he lost the *Call* job, he worked out a deal with his former boss, Joe Goodman, who was then still at the *Enterprise*, to write a daily article for that paper—the only stipulation being that the daily sub-mission should deal with life in San Francisco. The pay was to be thirty dollars a week. Twain was also reviewing plays for the *Dramatic Chronicle*, the only one of the newspapers of his time which survives in San Francisco today. (Nowadays, the *Dramatic Chronicle* is known as the San Francisco *Chronicle*.) The *Dramatic Chronicle* was paying Twain forty dollars a month for his services.

Of course, it was only natural that the first subject to which Twain addressed himself in the *Enterprise* was the brutal and corrupt San Francisco police department. He had been damming up so much information that he was unable to use while writing for the *Call*, that the minute he had an outlet for such things defamatory articles began spewing forth from his pen. As a result of the publication of these articles, the *Enterprise* began selling in San Francisco more briskly than ever before. The minute the paper arrived on the stage-coach from Virginia City, every available copy was snatched up by eager readers. Twain's name was suddenly on everyone's lips, and the controversy that was stirred up as a result of his exposé did not die down for a very long time. It remained to be seen whether or not Twain's attack on the police department would serve to attenuate the corruption there; but there was certainly no attenuation of Twain's reputation as a writer. Instead, his star began to rise rapidly in San Francisco's literary circles, and from there his fame gradually began spreading all over the Pacific Coast.

To understand the

effect that San Francisco's literary scene had on Mark Twain and on his writing, it is important for the reader to have a clear picture of just what that scene was. A great deal has been written about the cultural life of San Francisco during the 1860s, some of it lively and interesting, some of it dry and didactic. The Zeitgeist of that era, however, was anything but dull.

Probably the biggest cultural development of the nineteenth century was the emergence in the 1830s of the Bohemian movement. Originating in Paris and continuing in New York, nineteenth-century Bohemianism was a philosophy embracing Dionysian principles in an era of stern Calvinist morality. While the conventional wisdom of the era admonished its adherents to be circumspect, severe, frugal, and chaste, those who followed a Bohemian way of life joyfully drank to excess, flew in the face of prevalent sexual strictures, loudly proclaimed political opinions that were generally radical, and had a devil-may-care, communal attitude regarding living arrangements and money.

By the early 1860s, San Francisco had its share of transplanted New York Bohemians, an admittedly motley crew who were having varying effects on the California literary scene. California, for its part, had had quite an effect on these transplanted East Coast refugees, for it had grafted frontier pragmatism onto the basically Euro-

SLINKING.

pean Bohemian life style and literature, and the resulting mixture was both hardy and adventurous. The European-style Bohemianism that was flourishing in New York had, by the late 1850s, become too intent on hero worship, making the Bohemian scene in Greenwich Village almost a caricature of Parisian Bohemianism, with all its tubercular existentialism and wretched excesses. In San Francisco, however, this hothouse quality rapidly evaporated when it was exposed to the forthright no-nonsense attitudes of the growing pioneer city. The coming together of the seemingly disparate elements of European intellectualism and Pacific Coast empiricism ultimately created one of history's most exciting intellectual atmospheres. That hybrid was so vigorous that it has survived in some measure even until the present day; it is no accident that the beatnik and hippie movements of the 1950s and '60s were born in San Francisco, for example.

The literary San Francisco with which Mark Twain was familiar contained more colorful characters per square foot than anywhere else on earth, perhaps. There was Prentice Mulford, also known to his readers in the *Golden Era* as "Dogberry"–a cheerfully poverty-stricken recluse who lived on a shabby houseboat and wrote variously about mining, spiritualism, and the arts. Mulford was so shy that he sometimes waited for hours in the street near the *Golden Era*'s office, manuscript in hand, before he could get up the courage to walk in, even though he was one of the *Era*'s most popular contributors.

There was Ina Coolbrith, eventually California's first poet laureate, a young and lovely woman with a tragic secret past involving Mormonism (her uncle was Joseph Smith, the Latter-Day Saints' charismatic leader) and a marriage to a brutal drunkard in Los Angeles, which she had fled to San Francisco to escape. Coolbrith wrote a great deal of poetry, but she made her living as a librarian, first in Oakland (where she encouraged many young writers, including a young man from the wrong side of the tracks named Jack London), and finally at the Bohemian Club in San Francisco. She was reportedly involved romantically during the 1860s with both Mark Twain and Bret Harte, as well as with several other figures in San Francisco's literary scene.

There was Joaquin Miller, a fascinating bearded *poseur* fresh from the wilds of Oregon, whose literary beginnings in California were highly inauspicious—when Joe Lawrence, the editor of the *Golden Era*, looked over some of Miller's fledgling odes to the beauties of nature, he observed rather dryly that Miller should abandon versifying forthwith and return to Oregon to "grow taters." Miller persisted, however, and eventually became a patron saint of Bohemia in the Bay Area, serving in his old age as mentor to such second-generation Bohemians as George Sterling.

There was Adah Isaacs Menken, once described by Twain as his "fellow literary cuss"—a voluptuous *femme fatale* whose flamboyant histrionics predated those of future daughters of public tragedy such as Isadora Duncan. Menken considered herself an authoress, but her main claim to fame was as the chief attraction of a sensationalistic play called *Mazeppa*. During the finale, clad in nothing but a flesh-hued body stocking, she galloped across the stage tied to the back of a wild black stallion. Of her attempts at poetry, a single opening line should suffice: "Years and years the songless soul waited to drift out beyond the sea of pain where the shapeless life was wrecked."

And there was Bret Harte, with whom Mark Twain was to have a powerful lifelong love-hate relationship. When Twain had been the *Call's* "fading and perishing" reporter in the paper's third-floor offices, Bret Harte was one floor below him in the same building, serving as private secretary to the superintendent of the United States Mint. The mint, which was housed in a large and imposing structure at Fifth and Mission streets, had grown so crowded during the city's most recent flush period that it finally succeeded in squeezing out a number of its important employees, including the superintendent and his secretary. The superintendent had thus been obliged to take up new quarters in an annex in the *Call's* building. Harte had few duties as secretary to the superintendent, and he was able to spend the bulk of his work hours developing as a writer.

Harte's friendship with Twain began in the mint annex. The two men were of similar age—both being in their late twenties when they met—but there all similarity ended. Harte was a reserved and reticent fellow who had come west with his family from the Eastern Seaboard at the age of sixteen. The two writers were almost diametric opposites—Twain in disheveled attire, with brusque and blunt appraisals of everything from corrupt politicians to women who rejected his advances; and Harte, foppishly dressed, fond of elegant turns of phrase and epigrammatic wisdom. It was as if the raw and empirical Midwest, as embodied by Twain, had hit the East Coast, as typified by Harte, broadside.

At the time he met Twain, Harte's writing career was very much on the upswing. His short stories, with their views of life in California mining camps, were being turned out for the *Golden Era* and other journals, and were meeting with great success not only on the Pacific Coast but also in the East. Harte was extremely painstaking in his craftsmanship; he believed that he could create literature using the raw material of California's Gold Rush—an aim which Twain found as pretentious as it was preposterous. Twain had never had any fundamental use for "polite" literature, even in his early days; his language was the language of the common man, and when he chose to write about the Pacific Coast, he preferred to describe it in its own vigorous, unvarnished idiom. He thought Harte was too manipulative of his readers' emotions, and he would later dismiss Harte's renderings of colloquial speech in California as highly unnatural.

Yet when Twain first met Harte a friendship of sorts bloomed. Harte was famous in San Francisco literary circles for his ready wit and charm, and even though Twain would later castigate him because that wit was largely sarcastic, it is likely that Twain found Harte's sarcasm compatible with his own satirical side. Then, too, Harte seemed to have everything he himself lacked. In sharp contrast to the awkward bachelor Twain, who dreamed ruefully of lovely girls but was rarely successful with them, the sophisticated Harte not only had a wife, but was rumored to have a wealthy and generous mistress as well. Mrs. Harte was a former church soprano, and when he was at home, Harte's home life was conducted exactly according to those nineteenth-century standards Twain was later to ridicule in books such as *The Gilded Age*—while living that odious lifestyle himself. Harte also had something else which Twain dearly coveted—a literary future that looked extremely rosy.

In the early days of their friendship, Twain was eager to learn all he could from Harte, whose name served as an immediate entrée into San Francisco's prestigious literary circle. Twain's own reputation in San Francisco was distinctly nonliterary, and he greatly desired to advance beyond political reporting and oddball observations on civic events—even though those were often his strongest subjects. As dubious as Twain was about Harte's method of rendering California subjects acceptable to polite society, he was nonetheless willing to submit his own writing to Harte's scrutiny in order to develop into something more than a wandering (and mundane) newspaper reporter.

It must be admitted that Harte's literary discernment was considerable. He had, when Twain made his acquaintance, stopped contributing to the *Golden Era*, which he now dismissed as "narrow" and "provincial"—a view which was becoming increasingly popular among the *littérateurs* of San Francisco. Harte had worked his way up through the ranks on the *Golden Era*, starting as a typesetter and finally ending as the paper's most popular writer. As the author of a fashionable column, "The Bohemian Feuilleton," Harte had acquired a reputation as San Francisco's premier literary man-about-town; now, he explained to Twain, he wished to take that reputation elsewhere. Thus, he had, along with Charles H. Webb, just founded the *Californian*, a journal designed to appeal to a sophisticated San Francisco no longer satisfied with the rough-hewn frontier writing of the previous decade.

Largely because he respected Harte's literary judgement, if not his actual writing, Twain deferred to Harte and allowed him to edit his manuscripts. One of the most interesting things about Twain was his lifelong need to appoint somebody as his editor. In Nevada, it had been Joe Goodman; later it would be his wife, Olivia Clemens; and he also accepted personal editing, without flinching, from many others, qualified and otherwise, during his life. It was almost as if he needed someone to impose an external framework over him and explain to him what was right and what was wrong, in as arbitrary a manner as they wished. Early on, Twain seemed especially proud that Harte, the arch-man-of-letters in San Francisco, was willing to guide him in his writing. "Bret Harte trimmed and trained and schooled me patiently until he changed me from an awkward utterer of coarse grotesqueness to a writer of paragraphs and chapters that have found a certain favor in the eyes of even some of the very decentest people in the land," he was later to admit.

During the developmental phase of their friendship, Twain was also glad to spend time with Harte—first in the mint annex, until Smiggy McGlural came and the axe fell; and then in the various Bohemian haunts of San Francisco. One of their watering holes was

---

the home of Ina Coolbrith, the foremost female member of literary Bohemia. She was a gentle, supportive woman who was fond of giving dinners for her fellow writers, but she unwittingly caused quite a strain on Twain and Harte's friendship. Harte had always been fond of Coolbrith, and when he introduced Twain to her, Twain also was taken with her intelligence and charm. For a while the two friends vied for her affections, but she had apparently had enough of the slings and arrows of romance after her disastrous marriage in Los Angeles, at least for the time being, and she tactfully refused them both. Nonetheless, the two suitors were persistent, and the rivalry between them sometimes waxed hot indeed, as when Harte once appeared to be gaining a little ground with Coolbrith, however illusorily, and an infuriated Twain called him a name so vile that it has not been passed down to us.

THE *GOLDEN ERA*, WHICH

when Mark Twain met Harte, Harte had so recently abandoned, had been founded in the early 1850s. During the decade it had been in existence, it had served as the proving ground for nearly all of the Pacific Coast's writing talent. The newspaper's position in San Francisco's literary world had more to do with its sheer longevity than with the overall quality of its writing, for it was, as Harte had remarked, hardly a high-toned literary journal.

In both appearance and content, the *Era* was crude, presenting a conglomeration of local fiction and poetry, English translations of European novels and poetry, serialized works by such writers as Charles Dickens (the copyright laws were notoriously lax in those days), a smattering of local news, and various departments and columns. Readers of modern newspapers, who are accustomed to the large typefaces and relatively simple layouts of today's metropolitan dailies, would experience considerable eyestrain in poring over a typical editon of the *Golden Era*. Each issue contained eight pages of six columns each, printed on a grade of paper several steps below that used to print cheap journals such as the *Call*. The size of the *Era*'s type was so small that it has been estimated that one of its six-column pages carried about the same amount of printed matter as would thirty pages of an ordinary-sized modern book!

The *Era*'s contributors had included, over the years, all the colorful figures of San Francisco's literary Bohemia. Among them were Prentice Mulford, who wrote about mining under the pen name "Dogberry;" Artemus Ward, then America's most beloved homespun humorist and public lecturer; Adah Isaacs Menken, Ina Coolbrith, Joaquin Miller, Charles Warren Stoddard, and a surprisingly sweet-tempered young man named Fitzhugh Ludlow, whose book *The Hasheesh Eater*, about his strange odyssey through the world of exotic pharmacopeia, was causing a national stir.

The offices of the *Golden Era* were spacious and richly decorated in then-prevalent San Francisco style—red Turkish carpets, gold chandeliers, overstuffed sofas and chairs, and a general air of thoroughly bizarre opulence that would later be immortalized as "San Francisco Vulgar." Joaquin Miller described the *Era's* palatial headquarters thus: "The *Era* rooms were . . . the most grandly carpeted and most gorgeously furnished rooms that I have ever seen. . . . I have seen the world well since then . . . yet {the *Era's*} carpeted parlors, with Joe Lawrence and his brilliant satellites, outshine all things else, as I turn to look back."

The *Era's* proprietor, "Colonel" Joe Lawrence, was a genial host to all artistic and literary personages in San Francisco. He had built up his newspaper's reputation by forever being on the lookout for writing "names" to snag for publication—something at which he was generally successful. The cream of San Francisco's literary scene gravitated naturally to Lawrence, who charmed potential contributors over drinks at one of the city's lavish saloons. Lawrence's intellectual charm and his copious libations netted him many a first-rate contributor as well as many more who were somewhat less than first-rate.

But Lawrence was more than a socially gifted rake; he had good business sense, as well as a clear picture of the prevalent journalistic climate. He realized that even though San Francisco in its flush days was as freewheeling as any society could be expected to be, the Pacific Coast was nonetheless peopled by a great many settlers who had come from the Midwest, the South, and the East, and who still paid reverent homage to conventional nineteenth-century morality. For this reason, Lawrence understood that he had to strike some sort of balance between wild Bohemian literary ravings and more staid fare for those who preferred home spun homilies. Lawrence also never forgot that many of the *Era's* most faithful readers were not urban sophisticates but miners and farmers in the Sierra,

the Mother Lode country, and the Nevada Territory. For such readers, Lawrence had columns on mining and agriculture and other
down-to-earth subjects. This policy paid off handsomely as grateful
back-country subscribers faithfully renewed their subscriptions to
the *Era* year after year.

Many of Lawrence's contributors reflected this intriguing
combination of Bohemianism and just-plain-folksiness: Prentice
Mulford, for instance, with his Sag Harbor antecedents, his straight-
forward reportage on California mining, and his bizarre campaign for
the California State Assembly, during which, emboldened by too
much alcohol, he hurled surreal polemics at his would-be constitu-
ents. (He was not elected, but the margin was surprisingly narrow.)
Many of the *Era*'s female contributors also knew how to twang the
old homesteaders' heartstrings with rosy-cheeked poetry extolling
nursery, kitchen, and hearth—while at the same time some of them
were capable of tearing off Menkenian-style verse mourning for lost
lovers, weeping over broken hearts, exulting over tempestuous de-
sires, and the like.

In Mark Twain, these two elements—Bohemia and the frontier—were present in equal amounts. Born and reared in Missouri,
he already possessed the pragmatic, cracker-barrel stance common
to that part of the country; after meeting Bret Harte and becoming
involved in San Francisco's literary scene, he became increasingly
Bohemian in his outlook. In Virginia City, he had learned the newspaperman's trade; in San Francisco, however, under Harte's tutelage
and the influence of the literary scene, he went beyond journalistic
style and entered into the realm of pure ideas and philosophical
speculation.

Twain contributed to the *Golden Era* during his early days in
San Francisco, but then, along with the other literary lights of the
Pacific Coast, he made the switch to the *Californian*.

IT WAS ONLY LOGICAL THAT

sooner or later the less conventionally minded contributors to the
Golden Era would want to found a publication without the frontier
mentality that had served the *Era* so well for more than a decade.
Toward the end of their tenure on the *Era*, in fact, Bret Harte and
another *Era* columnist, Charles Webb, began joking in their columns
about the new paper they were going to establish. Webb, who

wrote under the pseudonym "Inigo," suggested that the new journal be called *Inigo's Christian Weekly Watchman*. Harte proposed that the forthcoming periodical be published entirely in French in order to show San Francisco how sophisticated and "literary" its publishing had become. Webb teased Harte in print, saying that since Harte was, after all, a married man, he would only be allowed to deal with the more homely of the future journal's female contributors. (Harte's schizophrenic private life, with his middle-class home and wild romantic escapades, was a much-discussed topic in literary circles.)

Webb and Harte unleashed the *Californian* in late May, 1864, just as Twain was arriving in San Francisco and was about to go to work for the *Call*. Webb served as the new paper's chief editor, and Harte was its primary contributor. Harte accordingly spent many a long hour at the mint annex writing articles and columns for the new paper, which impressed Twain mightily whenever he happened to step into Harte's office to pass the time of the day.

Harte soon persuaded Twain to shift his allegiance from the *Era* to the *Californian*, and Twain, who was anxious to become accepted as a full-fledged member of the city's *literati*—just as he had been eager in Virginia City to join the hard-drinking, hoax-loving brotherhood of sagebrush journalists on the *Enterprise*—readily acquiesced. Twain felt very keenly the stigma of being an itinerant reporter from the wilds of Washoe. There was a part of him that reveled in his reputation as "the Wild Humorist of the Pacific Slope"—a reputation that he had studiously cultivated in Nevada—but he was not completely comfortable with some of the less savory connotations that went with this image. From the moment he arrived in San Francisco, he took pains to seek out the company of clergymen, important government figures, and other respectable citizens, perhaps as a counterbalance to the company he kept in the city jail or in Barbary Coast saloons.

Therefore, when Harte began singing the praises of the *Californian*, Twain quickly saw that it would be advantageous to appear in its pages. Whereas the *Era* was a paper with an extremely regional outlook, the aura surrounding the *Californian* was cosmopolitan and sophisticated, and Twain wanted desperately to embody those qualities in his writing as well as in his personality.

When Twain had been contributing regularly to the *Californian* for four months, he wrote to his mother and sister in Hannibal, explaining about his weekly *Californian* articles. "I quit the *Era*, long ago," he said smugly. "It wasn't high-toned enough. The *Californian* circulates among the highest class of the community, and it is the best weekly literary paper in the United States."

His contributions showed that he was beginning to develop a jocular, loose-jointed style of writing, an approach he would refine but never completely abandon. In one of his weekly articles, he grumbled at great length about the discomfort of driving out to the Cliff House early in the morning; he admitted, however, to enjoying the view—filtered through the bottom of a whiskey glass. In another article, he announced, "Some people are not particular about what sort of company they keep. Now for several days I have been visiting the Board of Brokers, and associating with brokers, and drinking with them, and swapping lies with them, and being as familiar and sociable with them as I would with the most respectable people in the world." He then went on to describe the stockbrokers' peculiar lingo and some of the other goings-on at the Hall of the San Francisco Board of Brokers—better known, he pointed out, as the "Den of the Forty Thieves."

This sort of article, along with the blistering attacks on the police department that he was continuing to write for the *Enterprise*, show clearly how Twain's thinking was progressing from simple humor to moralizing and philosophy. Much to the amusement of sophisticates like Harte and Webb, Twain appeared to be almost feverishly anxious to remove all the remaining vestiges of "frontier humorist" from his writing reputation—even if it was to his own detriment. That Harte and Webb were tickled at Twain's awkward eagerness to become sophisticated overnight is clear; for a while, the *Californian* engaged in the pastime of publishing letters presumably written by various members of the San Francisco *literati*, in which each bogus "contributor" put in his or her application for the paper's editorship and specified what changes he or she would make in the paper's format. Harte and Webb had great fun exaggerating each "applicant's" tendencies, and the letter supposedly written by Twain was one of the funniest of the bunch. It was signed, "Yours, 'Mark Twain Surnamed The Moral Phenomenon'," and, poking fun at Twain's Presbyterian upbringing, it chastised the paper for supplying its readers with "too much wicked wit and too much demoralizing humor." "What the people are suffering for is Morality," trumpeted "Twain." "Turn them over to me . . . I can fetch them!"

Despite the fact that the *Californian* was well received all over the Pacific Coast and even made a few waves in that literary Parnassus, New York, it suffered from the severe financial ups and downs that literary journals invariably seem to encounter. The paper remained under the financial proprietorship of Charles Webb for only a few months; when finances grew shaky, Webb was forced to sell out to a group of printers to whom he owed money, although he continued to edit the paper. Harte remained as a steady contributor and major influence on the paper throughout its existence, and served as editor when Webb went on vacation.

The *Californian* survived only four years before it folded. Long after it was just a memory of the golden age of literature in San Francisco, Webb recalled, "The *Californian* nearly bankrupted me in an inconceivably short time." But the paper had served its purpose, for it had converted "the Wild Humorist of the Pacific Slope" into the "Moral Phenomenon" with one neat gesture, and it, along with the literary scene it represented, had also guided Mark Twain during a crucial formative period in his writing career. For his part, Twain would often look back on his *Californian* days with fondness and excusable nostalgia. More than once he was to refer to this period as "that old day when bohemianism was respectable – ah, more than respectable, heroic."

4
THE SECRET
LIFE OF
SAMUEL
CLEMENS

DURING THE TIME HE LIVED

in San Francisco, Mark Twain led the sort of life that many people look back on with fond longing in later, more restricted years. After he left the *Call*, Twain's hours were highly erratic, his day beginning when he rose at around 1 P.M. and ending whenever the last saloon on the Barbary Coast had closed, or when the conversation had finally degenerated into drunken snoring. Meanwhile, though, he was getting a great deal of writing done, often in marathon sessions during which he would lock himself in his room and produce three or four articles at a time.

The company he kept was of a mixed nature, running the gamut from clergymen to derelicts. The one constant in the ever-changing kaleidoscope of his acquaintances was Steve Gillis, with whom he roomed and with whom he often roamed abroad in the evenings. Twain and Gillis were insatiable in their continuing search for nocturnal excitement on the Barbary Coast, a search which was generally dedicated to finding a good pool table. When it came to the game of billiards, Twain was an out-and-out fanatic. He had acquired this addiction during his steamboating days, but it had increased tenfold while he was on the staff of the *Enterprise*. In Washoe, he had

DISSOLUTE AUTHOR.

pitted his cue against those of Dan De Quille, Joe Goodman, and the other *Enterprise* staffers, on the best tables the town had to offer, but in San Francisco he was able to rack up points on the most ornate and elaborately appointed tables he had ever seen. During that period in its history, San Francisco enthusiastically shared Twain's passion for billiards, and its gambling dens vied with one another in seeing who could purchase the most garishly designed and awe-inspiring pool table. Twain, a pretty fair player, was later to write at some length on the subject of billiards, calling it "the best game on earth" during a time when most of polite society considered the green felt to be the devil's very workshop. In the last, dark days of his life, he often turned to billiards as a solace, staying up all night and running game after game by himself in his study because his agitated mental state would not allow him to sleep. It is comforting to specu-late that, as he leaned over the table in those later years, Clemens may have recalled brighter days when he was footloose and unfet-tered on the Barbary Coast and his most serious problem was finding a gambling den that was open late enough.

Twain and Steve Gillis often terrorized nocturnal San Francisco in the company of a printer known as "Little Ward" who was even smaller and feistier than Gillis. Twain had never been one for physical combat, preferring instead to fight his battles with verbal vitriol. Ward and Gillis, on the other hand, were always on the lookout for a scrap, the tougher the better. One would imagine that there was no end of entertainment for the two pint-sized pugilists, for at night all the desperate adventurers, fly-by-nights, gamblers of all descriptions, and other soldiers of fortune came out of the woodwork and sallied forth seeking pleasure.

It was in a Turkish bath in the prosperous Montgomery Block that Twain met Tom Sawyer. Twain had acquired the spa vice in his Washoe days, when he could often be found in the steam room of Moritz's Bath House in Virginia City. His affinity for water has been expounded upon at some length by numerous biographers, so it needn't be recapitulated here. Suffice it to say that in San Francisco Twain fooled away many a pleasant hour in the gaudy bathing establishment on Montgomery Street. On one of his visits there, he fell into conversation with a gentleman named Tom Sawyer — that was his real name, or at least his real name at the moment. Sawyer and Twain became friends and, subsequently, poker partners. Some years later, when Twain had become a nationally famous author and had produced that wholesome children's classic, *Tom Sawyer*, Clemens's old bathhouse crony, who was then operating the most successful saloon in San Francisco, proudly posted a sign outside his establishment: "TOM SAWYER'S SALOON — THE ORIGINAL TOM SAWYER, PROP."

THE ONE THING THAT

seemed to be conspicuously absent from Twain's life at this point was romance. Not that Twain wasn't romantic. There was the rivalry with Harte over Ina Coolbrith, and another dalliance with a young and pretty Bohemian woman of letters, Lily Hitchcock, whom Twain would visit several years later in Paris, where she had gone to experience European Bohemianism in its birthplace. But Twain's eccentric personal habits, hot temper, and erratic hours, not to mention his lack of financial wherewithal, made him a questionable choice for a husband. As he said in a letter to an old school chum, Will Bowen, in Hannibal: "Marry be damned. I am too old to marry. . . . I have got gray hairs in my head." Then he added the final heartbroken comment: "Women appear to like me, but damn them, they don't love me."

They didn't love him because, frankly, Clemens presented some serious obstacles to marriage. For one thing, he viewed women with the unrealistic perspective so common to the Victorian era – he worshipped them, believing them to be ministering angels rather than human beings. From them he desired a governing hand and steady flow of maternal guidance in all matters, along with a funda‑ mental chasteness that even good Victorian lasses would be hard‑ pressed to live up to. Psychologically oriented writers have ob‑ served that when Twain eventually married, he married a woman who was almost a physical invalid; whatever significance this fact may have, it is true that Olivia Clemens was a staunch pillar of that Victorian propriety that her husband seemed so enraptured by. Bret Harte's wife was similar to Olivia Clemens in her conventionality and social narrow‑mindedness, and at one point, when his friend‑ ship with Harte was at a low ebb, Twain castigated Harte for being a poor husband, saying that Mrs. Harte was "in every respect Mrs. Clemens's peer."

Eventually Harte had caved in under the strain of so much re‑ sponsibility, and in essence he had abandoned his wife and children in order to live a peripatetic literary life. To his credit, he did con‑ tinue until his death to send home a goodly share of whatever he earned. Twain, however, was shocked and disgusted by what he perceived as Harte's callousness and insensitivity to family matters. In the bitter condemnation of Harte that Twain lingered over in his *Autobiography*, one senses a feeling of guilt – for Twain, too, for a variety of reasons, would be obliged to spend a fair amount of time exiled from his wife and daughters. Then, too, Clemens may have envied Harte his freedom even as he detested the basic indifference to marital obligations that had given him that luxury. The relation‑ ships of the two writers with their women definitely made up an im‑ portant part of their stormy relationship with one another.

There was another reason why Twain, like Kipling's elephant, was slow to mate. During his Mississippi steamboating days, Clemens had briefly made the acquaintance of a girl eight years his junior, Laura M. Wright, when she was a passenger on his boat. Their courtship, such as it was, was of very short duration, for she was traveling with her parents, and after she reached her destination there was no further contact between the two would-be lovers. Because Clemens was considerably older than Laura, who was little more than a child when he met her, her parents saw fit to sidetrack the budding romance by intercepting the letters Clemens sent to their daughter. Clemens, in turn, finally stopped writing to Laura when he realized she wasn't getting his correspondence. But even though the twenty-two-year-old Clemens put Laura Wright out of his conscious mind, he carried a torch for her unconsciously for the rest of his life. To him, she typified youth and purity and unconsummated affection—things which Twain always tended to wax rhapsodic over—and as a result she showed up in his dreams on occasions too numerous to recount. Over the years, he was to record in his various notebooks and journals that Laura had haunted his sleep in times and places as disparate as California's Mother Lode, when he was still a vigorous young man, and the New England of his old age. He was thinking of her often in San Francisco. A letter written to his

THE GRACE OF A KANGAROO.

mother during his Bohemian days tells a poignant story; in that letter, he asked with studied carelessness, "What has become of that girl of mine that got married? I mean Laura Wright."

WHEN IT CAME TO WRITING

about the vagaries of romance, Twain mingled humor and pathos with a deft hand. In a letter to his mother and sister, he recounted a comedy of errors involving himself and a young woman who was "a relative of Governor Stanford." This changeable specimen of femininity apparently kept him fascinated for a period of several weeks during which he never knew whether she would welcome him with a warm smile or just as readily freeze him with a chilling stare. Finally, he conceded in his letter, he had been forced to give up his roller-coaster courtship—it was just "too many for him."

Twain was also perfectly capable of poking hilarious fun at himself, or at least at a thinly disguised version of himself in the person of a young San Francisco reporter named John Brummel. Using his disastrous days on the *Call* as fodder, Twain began work on a play doomed to remain unfinished, which went by the name *Brummel and Arabella.* (He hoped, through theater connections obtained while reviewing plays for the *Dramatic Chronicle*, to see his creation produced, but other things caught his attention, and he never finished it.) The surviving fragment of the play reveals Brummel to be a bumbling, ineffectual fellow who can't keep his mind on anything for more than a few minutes at a time, and who is a perpetual chaser of news stories that never quite seem to pan out. He is also obsessed with longing for the object of his affections, Arabella Webster, who is keeping him from getting his work done. Brummel soliloquizes:

I'm thinking about her all the time—and I don't care what I'm writing—whether the item's about pigs, or poultry, or conflagrations or steamboat disasters, I manage to get her mixed into it somehow or other. How humiliating it was last night when the chief editor looked over my proof and wanted to know what Arabella Webster it was who was going to fight the prize fight with Rough Scotty the Kentucky Infant. And the day before I had her in three financial notices and drat it, for a week past they haven't sent a pack of old blisters to the county jail for getting on a bender and breaking things but what I've written up the item in a state of semi-consciousness and entire absent-mindedness and added my Arabella's name to the list. This won't do, you know. Some day I'll make a mistake and publish her as arrested for arson, or manslaughter, or shoplifting, or infanticide, or some other little eccentricity of the kind, and she'll notify me to inflict my company and my extraordinary attentions on somebody else.

What can be gathered from Twain's play is the fact that his life as a journalist in San Francisco was just too chaotic to permit him to enjoy the ordered pleasures of romance—at least conventional romance. It is true that there were those, such as Clemens's journalistic rival Albert Evans, who hinted darkly that Twain found solace (and consequently acquired a venereal disease) in a house of ill repute—a practice that was hardly uncommon in San Francisco at the time. If he did spend time with women of easy virtue, however, Twain never admitted it outright. One idly wonders whether this was because he considered the practice too common to occasion comment or, more likely, whether he was later concerned about the stigma attached to such a pastime in the convention-ridden world of the East Coast, and so made it a dark secret of his wayward past. The rumor did come back to haunt him a number of years later when he was courting hs future wife, Olivia Langdon, in Elmira, New York, but he managed to get around it somehow.

Still, Twain most definitely possessed a dark side to his personality, evinced by his marked fondness for drink and gambling, as well as by his fascination with ribald stories. In the circles in which he moved, patronizing houses of prostitution was certainly not unusual, so it is not unreasonable to surmise that he may have done so himself. It is a shame that those who knew Twain during his days on the Barbary Coast did not commit any succinct and reliable memories to print, for hard facts about Twain's sexual experiences and the effect they had upon him would no doubt shed light on some other murky areas of his life as well. Be that as it may, the cold hard facts have passed, unrecorded, into history; and all we have today are "Amigo's" journalistic attacks on Twain for consorting with prostitutes. It is an intriguing issue that will probably never be resolved— unless some previously unknown document detailing Twain's sexual life suddenly surfaces, which is not very likely.

CONTINUING HIS CAMPAIGN

to correct San Francisco's corrupt government from the pulpit of the press, Twain lost no opportunity to hurl abuse at the local police from the columns of the *Enterprise*. The fact that he was correct in his assessment of the force's corruption was no protection, and eventually, after several Twain articles had appeared in the *Enterprise*, the chief of police, Martin G. Burke, filed a libel suit against the paper. This goaded Twain into responding with another, more blistering attack in the *Enterprise*, in which he accused the police of aiding and abetting lecherous practices in the city by turning a (paid-for) blind eye to them. He was fully aware of the danger inherent in such topics; on the envelope in which he mailed the article to Virginia City, he scrawled a note to the *Enterprise* print shop: "Be sure and let Joe see this before it goes in." When Goodman read Twain's scarifying attack, his only reply was, "Let it all go in, every word. If Mark can stand it, I can."

This was the state of affairs when Twain became involved in an unfortunate situation with Steve Gillis. Shortly after the lawsuit had been initiated against the *Enterprise*, Gillis was on his way home from work at the *Call* when he spotted a saloon brawl taking place on Howard Street. As has been mentioned, Gillis loved nothing better than the prospect of throwing himself into a fray, and on closer inspection, this one turned out to have elements that made getting involved in it worthwhile. Apparently the saloon's proprietor, a ruffian called Big Jim Casey, had just settled back to watch a muscular thug make mincemeat out of another fellow, a small and defenseless party who just happened to be an enemy of Casey's.

Gillis knew the principals in this little drama, and when he had ascertained the scenario, he promptly joined the proceedings in defense of the underdog. Big Jim, of course, did not take very kindly to this completely unexpected interruption in the evening's festivities, so he stepped in and broke up the fight, allowing the underdog to crawl away, very much shaken. Then Casey locked the front door to the saloon, put the only key in his pocket, and turned to face Gillis. "Now, Mister, since you've butted in without being asked, I'll finish the job on you," he snarled, lunging at Gillis. But Steve managed to snatch a large, heavy glass beer pitcher off the bar, and the minute the enraged Casey got within striking distance, Gillis hit him over the head with the massive object. They certainly don't make cut glass like they used to, for as a result of the blow the big bruiser crumpled onto the sawdust-covered floor, unconscious.

Steve Gillis now attempted to leave the scene of the crime, but it wasn't possible. The key to the door was stuck in Casey's pocket, and the massive Casey was lying on it. Gillis was still standing in front of the long mahogany bar, feverishly pondering possible avenues of escape, when two constables broke down the door in response to a call. Seeing Big Jim lying on the floor with blood streaming copiously from his scalp, the officers arrested Gillis first and elected to ask questions later. He was conveyed roughly and unceremoniously to the police station, where he was charged with assault and battery and locked up until somebody should arrive to bail him out.

That task fell to Mark Twain, Gillis's closest friend. When he heard that Gillis was behind bars, Twain managed to scrape together the five hundred dollars needed for his bail. Then, with a considerable number of vile curses and other fancy language, Twain dragged Gillis home, all the while continuing to blast him for getting into such a scrape. Didn't Gillis realize how precarious a position Twain was going to be in, what with the lawsuit? Gillis mildly accepted Twain's chastisement, although he didn't promise never to do it again—that would have been contrary to his nature.

The next day, Twain and Gillis received a piece of news that made their blood run cold—Big Jim Casey's condition had worsened, and he was raving deliriously over in the county hospital. Those in the know were speculating that the next saloon Casey would be operating would be located somewhere on the outskirts of the Elysian Fields—if he wasn't dispensing drink in a warmer climate. To make things infinitely worse, Casey was an especial friend of Chief of Police Burke, the fellow who had taken such a strong dislike to Twain and the *Enterprise*. Thus, when Casey kicked the bucket, as he surely would, both Twain and Gillis would be in hot water up to their respective necks—that much was crystal clear.

Upon reflection, Gillis reluctantly decided to become a bail jumper. He would abscond to Virginia City and resume his old typesetting job on the *Enterprise*. As for Clemens, the pleasures of San Francisco were becoming a little contemptible from over familiarity, so he planned to take an enforced vacation to avoid implication in the charges of Gillis's bail jumping as well as some of the more undesirable recreations that might result from the lawsuit. Steve's older brother Jim Gillis happened to be visiting in San Francisco at the time of the Casey episode, and he graciously offered Twain sanctuary in his cabin in the Mother Lode country on the Stanislaus River. Twain was happy to acquiesce—after nearly a year of fighting corruption in city government as well as in himself, he was ready for a change of scenery. So, on December 4, 1865, he took up his residence in Jim Gillis's cabin on Jackass Hill in California's Mother Lode country.

5
THE SOCIETY
UPON THE
STANISLAUS

IN HIS OWN WAY, JIM GILLIS

was quite literary. Over the years his little cabin in the rolling hills of California's mining country had served as a retreat for a number of city-weary writers, one of whom had been Bret Harte, who spent a brief period living in the cabin at a time when he was ill, broke, and discouraged about his future. Jim Gillis had lent Harte twenty dollars and advised him to try his luck on a San Francisco newspaper, which Harte did. A few months later, during a visit to San Francisco, Gillis found out where Harte was living and decided to pay him a friendly visit just to see how he was getting on. Harte, however, took offense at Gillis's visit; he assumed that Gillis was merely trying to collect the twenty dollars he had previously lent him. Consequently, he sent Gillis away rather perfunctorily, refusing to listen to him when he tried to explain that he had written off the debt and just wanted to congratulate Harte on the fact that he seemed to be making a successful career for himself in the city.

Gillis's cabin, on Jackass Hill near Angels Camp, was a few miles away from the mining towns of Tuttletown and Sonora, surrounded by sighing pines and in full view of the regal Sierra Nevada mountain range with its ever-changing light and shadow. Down out of the Sierra tumbled and rolled the great Stanislaus River, which was to be immortalized in "The Society Upon the Stanislaus" and other writings of Bret Harte. Twain later recalled the area as "that serene and reposeful and dreamy and delicious sylvan paradise."

Twain described Gillis's cabin as follows in the journal he was keeping at the time: "No planking on the floor; old bunks, pans and traps of all kinds—Byron, Shakespeare, Bacon, Dickens & every kind of only first class literature." This last was a reference to Gillis's extensive library, for, as well as writing a little himself, the elder Gillis was an avid reader. In this he resembled other California "sourdoughs," for their seemingly rough and illiterate ranks contained many a self-styled philosopher and idiot savant.

Jim Gillis and Mark Twain shared Gillis's cabin with a miner named Dick Stoker, whose fictitious cat, "Tom Quartz," was to make an appearance in Twain's *Roughing It*. Jim Gillis's younger brother William, called Billy by the cabin's various tenants, was also staying in the cabin during the time Twain lived there.

The area surrounding Angels Camp had been a populous mining settlement during the flush period of the 1850s, but by the time Twain took up his abode on Jackass Hill, there was only a handful of dilapidated cabins standing on the spot where twelve or fifteen years earlier a vital, thriving boomtown had been conducting its bustling daily business. This fact made quite an impression on Twain, for it symbolized just how mercurial life and fortune on the Pacific Coast could be. The ghostly ruins of Angels Camp caught Twain's fancy as he loafed and dreamed among them; it seemed to him that the dead mining camp, with its lost and bygone air, suited his present mood exactly.

Jim Gillis, Dick Stoker, and the few remaining miners in the area engaged in what was known as "pocket" mining—a process that was unique to that one little corner of California, at least as far as Twain knew. After spending a few months in the apparent capital of pocket mining, Twain was to claim that it was the most fascinating style of mining he had ever witnessed—perhaps, as he observed, because, due to its extreme uncertainty, pocket mining furnished a large number of victims to the lunatic asylum.

The theory behind pocket mining was that in this particular part of California, gold was scattered at random throughout the soil, and the only thing needed to pinpoint precisely where it lay was a

JIM GILLIS'S CABIN ON JACKASS HILL IN CALIFORNIA'S
MOTHER LODE COUNTRY. THE CABIN SEEN HERE LATER BURNED
DOWN, AND A NEW ONE WAS BUILT AROUND THE ORIGINAL
STONE CHIMNEY, WHICH SURVIVED THE FIRE.

systematic method. The pinpointing was accomplished through a tedious process of panning the soil in random increments. Perhaps a few panfuls of soil, when rinsed with water, would reveal tiny flecks of gold; if so, then the prospector would try samples from either side of the lucky strike to narrow down his field of search. By this process of elimination, the miner would eventually hope to locate the section where the most gold was concentrated. It was by nature extremely time-consuming, and the constant uncertainty of the proceedings was what Twain believed sent the victims to the loony bin. Some-times a pocket miner could strike one initial shovelful of gold and then never come up with any more after that, no matter how dili-gently he worked. There were, however, some real reasons for Gillis, Stoker, and the other speculators to keep up their hard work— one strike, for instance, had been made in the area not long before Twain arrived that had totaled $60,000 worth of gold. It had taken

THE MINER'S DREAM.

Mark Twain in California

two men two weeks to dig out the bonanza. (They had then sold the excavation site for $10,000 to another fellow who, according to Twain, never got fifty dollars out of it afterward.)

Twain was as fascinated as ever with the concept of sudden wealth, but his energy was at a low ebb and he was content to leave the physical work of mining to those with broader shoulders and fewer qualms about labor than he. His cabinmates loved to rib him about his lassitude, which was becoming almost legendary among those who knew him. Sometimes Jim Gillis would needle him about the time back in Virginia City when Twain had been reading in bed and his ever-present pipe had gone out. Rather than get up and walk two or three feet to where the matches were sitting, Twain had waited until his roommate, Dan De Quille, had come home a few hours later, whereupon Twain had asked him for a light.

Twain thoroughly enjoyed Jim Gillis's company, and Gillis was even able, on one or two occasions, to persuade his sluggish friend to pitch in and do some mining. On one such occasion—recollected by Albert B. Paine in his biography of Twain—Clemens and Gillis trudged up a hill to a likely site during a chilly, drizzly afternoon. Once they began working, Gillis, who was well versed in the vagaries of pocket mining, became convinced that they were about to make a big strike any minute. Twain was less sure, but arguing took too much effort, so he kept his doubts to himself. His job was to fetch water from a stream that was flowing at the foot of the hill; the water was then used to wash the pans of dirt. As the afternoon progressed, each pan looked more promising than the one before it, but by the time evening began to fall there still had been no payoff, and meanwhile Twain was shivering miserably and his teeth were chattering as the drizzle began to soak through his clothes. Finally he drawled at Gillis, "Jim, I won't carry any more water. This work is too disagreeable."

Poor Gillis was just about to wash out another pan of soil when he received this bombshell. "Bring one more pail, Sam," he said pleadingly.

But Twain flatly refused, explaining that he was freezing and felt like giving up. In vain did Gillis repeat his request in a beseeching tone of voice. "Just one more pail, Sam?"

Twain was adamant. "No, sir, not a drop, not even if I knew there were a million dollars in that pan."

STRIKING A POCKET.

Sadly, Gillis ceased laboring, for he couldn't simultaneously fetch water and wash dirt by himself. After the two men first posted the required thirty-day claim at the site, they then walked back to the cabin.

The weather prevented them from engaging in any more prospecting on the site, and they soon moved on to other locations and forgot about the hillside claim altogether. Meanwhile, the rain had washed away the topsoil in the pan of earth they had left behind them at the claim—the pan which Twain had refused to fetch the water to wash. Under the topsoil in that pan, as it turned out, was a handful of solid gold nuggets.

This was naturally bound to catch the eye of miners more enterprising than Mark Twain. Two Austrians happened along, spied the glittering lure in the pan, and sat down to wait until Gillis's thirty-day claim had expired. As soon as it had, they began panning the surrounding earth with great expectations. Two or three pans of dirt later they struck a pocket of nuggets. By the time they had cleaned out the pocket, they were twenty thousand dollars richer.

Twain was always extremely eloquent in the matter of self-deprecation. It would have been very interesting indeed to hear the names he called himself when he found out that one more lousy pail of water hauled uphill would have freed him from journalistic drudgery for the rest of his life.

In san francisco, Clemens

had been accustomed to dining on scalloped oysters and champagne beneath the gilt chandeliers of elegant, quasi-European restaurants. In Angels Camp the victuals were bound to be considerably less refined. He made the following note in his journal: "Jan. 23, 1865 – Angels – Rainy, stormy – Beans & dishwater for breakfast at the Frenchman's; dishwater & beans for dinner, and both articles warmed over for supper."

After a few more days of rain, beans, and dishwater, his grumbling took on a somewhat brighter note: "26th – Tapidaro [he meant tapadera, the leather stirrup covering on a saddle] beefsteak for a change – no use, could not bite it.

"28th – Chili beans & dishwater three times to-day, as usual, & some kind of 'slum' which the Frenchman called 'hash.' Hash be damned."

There was a happy ending, of sorts.

"30th Jan. – Moved to new hotel, just opened – good fare, & coffee that a Christian may drink without jeopardizing his eternal soul."

Twain found the small local population of Angels Camp just as unrefined as the cuisine. Not surprisingly, he was often bored to tears by the local goings-on. "The exciting topic of conversation in this sparse community just at present," he noted sourly in his journal, "(and it always *is* in dire commotion about something or other of small consequence), is Mrs. Carrington's baby, which was born a week ago, on the 14th. There was nothing remarkable about the baby, but if Mrs. C had given birth to an ornamental cast-iron dog big enough for an embellishment for the State-House steps I don't believe the event would have created more intense interest in the community."

The only locals Twain could tolerate were a nearby family with two young and comely daughters, Molly and Nelly Daniels, who were known in the area as "the Chaparral Quails." Twain and

Billy Gillis often paid formal calls on the girls, and the foursome sometimes took walks along the deserted trails that disappeared into the hills. On one of these occasions, the party got lost in those hills and came straggling home to the girls' cabin at an hour that was too late to be considered proper. The girls' mother assailed them at the door with a massive outpouring of opinion about heedless rakes such as Clemens, who would stoop so low as to seduce young and innocent girls in cow pastures. Twain wisely refused to involve himself in this one-sided conversation, and walking over to a corner of the cabin, he picked up a guitar that was leaning against the wall and proceeded to sing and play a few folk songs called forth from memory. (Twain always loved indigenous music, especially Negro spirituals, which he had heard from birth.) The girls' mother was so thoroughly enchanted by this impromptu performance that she wound up cooking a late supper for the prodigal Twain, Billy Gillis, and her daughters.

With the exception of the Chaparral Quails, Twain distinctly preferred the company of his cabinmates to that of the locals, however. One of the things he enjoyed the most about living on Jackass Hill was listening to Jim Gillis tell tall tales in front of the fireplace on chilly afternoons and evenings. Gillis would stand there reflectively,

DRINKING SLUMGULLION.

---

with his hands crossed behind him and his back to the fire, and pro-
ceed to relate elaborate and ultimately implausible tales, usually fea-
turing Dick Stoker as their hero. Meanwhile Stoker would be sitting
quietly in a corner, smoking his pipe and nodding serenely as Gillis
painted him in increasingly fantastic lights. One of Gillis's yarns was
retold by Twain in *Roughing It* – it was about the remarkable sagacity of Stoker's cat, Tom Quartz. It didn't matter that Stoker did not
own a cat and had never owned one; Gillis went on describing the
feline's perspicacity in mining as if the animal was still fresh in his
mind from yesterday. Another Gillis tale, "The Tragedy of the Burning Shame," was retold by Twain in *Huckleberry Finn*; Twain regret-
ted that he had to clean up the yarn considerably to make it fit for
publication. "This was a great damage," he mourned in his *Autobiography*. "As Jim told it, inventing it as he went along, I think it was one
of the most outrageously funny things I have ever listened to. How
mild it is in the book and how pale; how extravagant and how gorgeous in its unprintable form!"

Another California tall tale that Twain used to good advan-
tage was a long, monotonous narrative about a contest between two
hayseeds to ascertain which of two frogs could jump the farthest. It
was hardly a new story, even though Twain first chanced to hear it
in the Mother Lode; in actuality, it dated back to Aristophanes, and
in more recent years it had appeared in several Pacific Coast newspapers in various permutations and guises. But when Twain first
heard the dull, rambling fable drop ever so slowly from the lips of a
loquacious old gent in a decrepit tavern on Jackass Hill, what ap-
pealed to him was the manner in which the story was told.

Twain and Jim Gillis, with or without Dick Stoker, were fond
of playing billiards or just sitting around the potbelly stove in the
dreary old tavern, part of an equally dreary hotel owned by the same
Frenchman whom Twain had reviled for doling out the execrable
beans and dishwater. The wintry weather was keeping Twain and
his friends from getting around much, so they welcomed the chance
to play billiards on the tavern's rickety table, or to shoot the breeze
with whatever indiscriminate company happened to stop in for a
drink.

Twain was always to remember the slanting, battered relic of
a pool table in the Angels Camp tavern with great affection. In his
old age his fancy sometimes returned to the table's torn felt and un-

dulating surface, and the chipped pool balls and headless cues, the latter with curves in them like parentheses. Once, when Twain and his cabinmates saw their fellow tavern habitué, Texas Tom, rack up a whopping total of seven points during a single inning, they all went mad with admiration and amazement—the table was that difficult to score on.

Another inmate of the decaying saloon was a former Illinois river pilot named Ben Coon, a dim-witted, solemn fellow who dozed by the stove most of the time and was given, when awake, to delivering endless, pointless monologues. Twain and Gillis, bored and bereft of outside influences much of the time, found Coon amusing under the circumstances, and Twain was further tickled by the fact that Coon's run-on narratives never seemed to have a focal point. Later, Twain would write on several occasions about people to whom all details were of equal importance. It is likely that the grand-daddy of all these infuriating characters was the self-important Ben Coon.

One raw and dreary afternoon, Ben Coon took his usual seat by the stove and began droning on about a frog belonging to some man named Coleman. Coleman, it seemed, had trained this frog to jump on command, but when he tried to pit it against another frog, the rival's owner secretly loaded Coleman's amphibian with buck-shot, weighing it down and causing it to lose the contest. This was a witless enough story, and Coon had in all probability stumbled across it in one of the backwoods weekly newspapers that reached the area at odd intervals, or could even have heard it on the river. But it was Coon's uniquely irritating delivery rather than the yarn itself that struck Twain as noteworthy. He jotted down the bare bones of the story in his notebook, intending to go back to it at some point and write it up more fully. "Coleman with his jumping frog—bet stranger $50—stranger had no frog, & C got him one—in the mean-time stranger filled C's frog full of shot & he couldn't jump—the stranger's frog won."

There is no doubt that the period Twain spent in the Mother Lode was extremely fruitful in his development as a writer. The editors of his notebooks and journals (University of California Press, Berkeley) have pointed out that the notebook Twain kept while living in Jim Gillis's cabin on Jackass Hill, despite its brevity, contains material that Twain was to make use of throughout his literary career. None of his other notebooks bears that distinction. (The Mother Lode notebook contains some other irregularities—namely, some abortive attempts at shorthand in the various entries, and a considerable number of French words and phrases. Twain apparently taught himself a fair amount of French while living on Jackass Hill; he practiced it on the Frenchman of the decrepit tavern and the horrible hash.)

In his Mother Lode notebook, Twain set down a number of humorous anecdotes in their sketchiest forms, varying details here and there as if he were trying to see how to best squeeze the humor from the stories. One of these entries, which he called "Report of Prof. G— to accompany Map & Views of the Great Vide Poche Mine, on Mount Olympus, Calaveras Co.," was a full-blown short article written, as the title suggests, in the form of a report by some erstwhile mining expert (very likely Jim Gillis) to an undisclosed committee. Twain may have intended to read it to the nightly gathering in the cabin. He always enjoyed satirizing legalese and judicial language, and this burlesque managed to cram a fair amount of pompous-sounding verbiage into a very limited space. At one point, "Professor G—" was forced to admit that "The map is not absolutely correct. . . . [A]t the time the Prof was drawing it, seated upon a log, he was persistently besieged by piss-ants." The mine's outcroppings were described as containing nearly every mineral known to man—

some soapstone, some brimstone, & even some jackstones, whetstones, 'dobies & brickbats. None of these various articles are found beneath the surface, wherefore the Prof feels satisfied that the [mining] Company have got the world by the ass, since it is manifest that no other organ of the earth's frame could possibly have produced such a dysentery of disorganized & half-digested slumgullion as is here presented.

Although his public humor was developing apace, Twain himself remained absolutely humorless when he himself was the target of satire. Billy Gillis recalled many years later that one of the favorite pastimes in the Gillis cabin during long evenings was a game in which the "boys" implemented a "Hospital for the Insane" on Jackass Hill. A "board of directors" and "resident physician" were appointed, and reports on particular "patients" were made weekly to the committee by the "physician." When Twain's turn as "physician" rolled around, he expressed his grave and fatherly concern about the condition of James N. Gillis,

a companionable young fellow [who] tells some fairly humorous stories. . . . [I]t is sad to know that this young man, who would otherwise be a useful member of society, is hopelessly insane, but such, I am sorry to say, is the truth. He is laboring under the illusion that he is the greatest pocket miner on earth . . . and the only miner having a perfect knowledge of gold-bearing ledges and formations. He is a fairly good pocket hunter and knows a gold nugget from a brass door knob, but there are a dozen boys on the hill who can give him cards and spades and beat him at the game.

Jim Gillis laughed just as hard as the others at this "report." The next week, however, it was his turn to be the "physician," and he addressed himself to the problematic case of inmate Samuel L. Clemens.

One of the most pitiful cases of insanity that has ever fallen under my observation is that of a young man named Samuel L. Clemens, who was committed to this hospital on the thirteenth day of last month, from Angels Camp, Calaveras County. . . . He has, for the past three years, been associated with newspapermen of rare literary ability. He is obsessed with the idea that they are the spokes of a wheel and himself the hub around which they revolve. He has a mania for story telling, and is at the present time engaged in writing one entitled "The Jumping Frog of Calaveras," which he imagines will cause his name to be handed down to posterity from generation to generation as the greatest humorist of all time. This great story of his is nothing but a lot of silly drivel about a warty old toad that he was told by some joker in Angels Camp. Every evening when the inmates are together in the living room, he takes up the manuscript and reads to them a page or two of the story. . . . Then he will chuckle to himself and murmur about "copyrights" and "royalties." If this was the only trouble with Mark Twain, as he dubs himself in his stories, there would be a reasonable hope of the ultimate restoration of his mentality, but the one great hallucination that will forever bar him from the "busy walks of life" is that he was at one time a pilot on one of the great Mississippi River packets. . . . Poor Mark! His nearest approach to being a pilot on the river was when he handled the big steering wheel of a flat boat, freighted with apples from Ohio, which were peddled in towns along the river.

All the "boys" exploded with mirth—all of them, that is, but Samuel Clemens. He was livid with rage. He leaped to his feet and paced back and forth, flinging out fiery sarcasms at Gillis, and calling the others "a lot of laughing jackals." "I appreciate a joke," he sputtered, "and love fun as much as any boy in the world, but when a lot of rotten stuff like Jim Gillis's funny hash is pulled off on me I am ready to cry quits." As a result of Clemens's extreme displeasure, the "asylum" was closed down permanently, although the "boys" continued to take little pokes at Twain just to hear him rage and curse. "Say, Sam, how many barrels of apples could you load onto that flat-bottomed scow?" they would wickedly ask, and then quickly look around for something to hide behind. In his book, *Memories of Mark Twain and Steve Gillis*, Billy Gillis observed that when Twain was angry at someone, instead of talking the incident over in a calm and friendly way, he generally grabbed a drill, pick handle, or any other weapon that came handy and brained the offender with it. Luckily, Twain's rages died down as quickly as they flared up, and then he would be likely to suffer great feelings of remorse, although he often found it difficult to apologize to the wronged party.

Twain apparently never lost his sensitivity to humor aimed in his direction. An old newspaper clipping from the Carson City *Appeal*, dating back to the 1870s or 1880s, reveals a side of Twain that his readers may never have realized existed. The clipping, which reposes in the files of the Mark Twain Papers in Berkeley, contains a farfetched and tongue-in-cheek story about how Twain and Dan De Quille had decided to start a newspaper in Mendocino County during the 1860s. Twain and De Quille had, according to the clipping, taken all the type and other printing equipment "from a recently-defunct newspaper establishment in San Francisco" with which they had presumably been involved, and had headed off to Mendocino to establish a newspaper there. En route, they had stopped and purchased a small cannon from "a party of emigrants" they met, and had then continued on until they finally were forced to stop for the night in a cheerless wilderness area. Late that night (the story goes on) they were attacked by hordes of marauding Indians, and Twain, thinking quickly, jumped up and loaded the cannon with "a column of nonpareil and a couple of sticks of young spring poetry," along with some other boilerplate rubbish, which, when shot forth from the cannon, blew the oncoming attackers sky-high and just saved the lives of Twain and De Quille by an apostrophe.

Anyone reading this old clipping can see how broad the humor in it is. It starts off in a serious enough tone, but by the time the article's anonymous author has the now-famous Twain writing De Quille a letter, years later, from his home in Hartford, Connecticut, asking De Quille to "make a little pilgrimage to that historic spot, gather the ghostly relics together and plant a tablet, not too expensive and at your expense, for the memory of the departed," it is impossible not to chuckle at the sly but affectionate pokes some old fellow reporter is taking at Twain. Yet it appears that Twain took the clipping at face value, for scrawled across its length is a message in his handwriting, in purple ink: "Pure imagination—not a fact in it. SLC."

DURING TWAIN'S STAY WITH

Jim Gillis, he frequently visited other parts of the Mother Lode. One place where he and Gillis spent a fair amount of time was Calaveras County. There Gillis continued his pocket mining and Twain, as usual, sat nearby and supervised.

On New Year's Eve in the Calaveras County town of Vallecito, Twain recorded in his notebook that he had seen a "magnificent lunar rainbow," which he glimpsed through a light, pattering rain and that he took to be an auspicious omen of future good fortune. Little did he know that his Mother Lode experiences were about to change his life in ways he couldn't possibly have forseen.

6
A "VILLAINOUS BACK-WOODS SKETCH" IN PARNASSUS

AFTER SPENDING THREE

months of fruitful solitude there, Mark Twain left the Mother Lode country in February, 1865. He had bidden Jim and Billy Gillis and Dick Stoker farewell and was riding away when he discovered that he had left his toothbrush, his pipe, and his pocket knife in Angels Camp. With much swearing he was obliged to return and "smouch" Dick Stoker's knife.

He headed on horseback for the boomtown of Copperopolis, twelve miles from Jackass Hill, where he could catch the stage to Stockton and thence to San Francisco. Once in Copperopolis, he toured the local copper mines, which were famous for producing the most copper of any mines in the United States. To his disgust, however, he found that the stage into Stockton would not be leaving that day; he would have to wait until the following morning. Twain accordingly spent the night in the town's hotel, which he dismissed in his notebook as "damned poor," and, catching the stage in the morning, he was in Stockton by 5 P.M. the next day and in San Francisco on the day after, the twenty-sixth of February, at which time he checked into the Occidental Hotel—his old "heaven on the entire shell."

As he was signing in, the desk clerk handed him some mail that had come for him during his absence from San Francisco. One of the letters was from Artemus Ward, an old friend of his. Ward was then at the peak of his fame as a humorist, with capacity audiences across the country lining up to hear him give public lectures such as "Babes in the Woods." He had an equally large following for his humorous writings in newspapers and magazines. Among other things, Ward had popularized the use of an exaggeratedly illiterate backwoods dialect that he used to good ironic and humorous effect in his writing.

In Virginia City during the winter of 1863–64, Twain and Dan De Quille and the other jolly good fellows from the *Enterprise* had engaged in a massive orgy of alcoholic good cheer with Ward, helping him celebrate a triumphant lecture tour of California and Nevada. The binge was of such duration and intensity that it had become imperishably engraved in Pacific Coast history. Twain had reportedly been the last man on his feet late in the afternoon on New Year's Day, 1864, after some three weeks of serious drinking, indiscriminate socializing, congratulatory speeches, and general backslapping. In the back room of Virginia City's finest bar, Twain had raised the only crystal goblet left in one piece after the previous evening's festivities, and to his dear friend Ward, snoring obliviously with his head on an empty magnum bottle of Mumm's champagne, he had proposed a final toast: "To Artemus Ward, first in bars, first in pieces, first –" And then he too had collapsed amidst the broken glasses, overturned plates of half-eaten delicacies, and magnificent disarray.

Since Twain had left Virginia City, he hadn't seen much of Ward, but Ward kept tabs on how his friend's career was going and tried to give Twain a boost whenever he could. Now Twain discovered that Ward wanted him to send a humorous sketch for a book he was putting together. The only problem was that Ward's letter was dated the previous November. It appeared to be too late for Twain to fill Ward's request.

In Virginia City, Ward, who hailed from the East Coast and continued to make his home there, had often told Twain that he felt he had great literary talent, and that all he needed to do to establish a national reputation was to clean up his act a little. Ultimately, Ward argued, Clemens should take up his residence in New England, where all men of letters ought to live. On the face of it, this was rather strange advice from a man who had made his own reputation pretending to be an illiterate backwoodsman (for Ward did not come from that background), but perhaps Ward detected Clemens's own contradictory desire to be accepted by polite society even while he was ridiculing the morals of the good ladies of Carson City and at the same time occasionally passing out in Virginia City doorways from a surfeit of good cheer. At any rate, Ward was now requesting a piece of humorous Californiana from Twain with an eye toward alerting the East Coast reading public to Clemens's existence.

Twain saw the advantages to be derived from appearing in an anthology compiled by Ward, and he quickly wrote Ward a reply, explaining that he had been away from San Francisco during December, January, and February, but that he would send something along immediately. Then he went to work writing up the jumping-frog story he had heard Ben Coon rattle off in Angels Camp. Unfortunately, Twain was told his story arrived in New York too late to be included in Ward's book. Ward's publisher, George Carleton of Carleton and Co., gave the sketch to Henry Clapp, the editor of a popular national magazine, the *Saturday Press*, and Clapp published it there.

At the time he wrote the story that was to be known to future generations as "The Celebrated Jumping Frog of Calaveras County," Mark Twain was extremely popular and well known all over the Pacific Coast, but his writing had not yet crossed the Rockies. The San Francisco literary scene of which he was an integral part was still in the process of developing, and although its writers would one day take their rightful places among Eastern men and women of letters, the San Franciscans were at that point only a regional phenomenon, with no reputation outside California and Nevada.

Twain's position in San Francisco's literary world at this time was equal to that of Bret Harte, but no one was prophesying that he would one day be idolized as the greatest writer ever produced by the United States. Still, it is likely that Twain was eager to spread his name and his writing all over the country, for then as now a national literary reputation could not be attained by limiting one's activities to the West Coast. From this end of time, "The Jumping Frog" seems to be more of a caricature of life in a Mother Lode mining town than a real-life rendering. It is almost as if Twain had been trying to portray a cartoonish, unreal California, peopled with rustic oafs and buffoons, in order to win praise from Artemus Ward, with his typical Easterner's view of the uncivilized Pacific Slope as a literary way station.

There is some possibility that Carleton, Ward's publisher, did not like the story, for as a result of the rejection of "The Jumping Frog," there was bad blood between Carleton and Clemens for a number of years. However, the book, a collection of "Nevada Territory Travels," was not fated to go down in history. The only reason anyone remembers it at all today is because it did not include "The Celebrated Jumping Frog of Calaveras County." Twain was plainly aware of the book's faults. In a letter to his mother and sister, he remarked that Ward's book "was a wretchedly poor one, generally speaking, and it could be no credit to either of us to appear between its covers."

Fate was far kinder to the frog yarn that it was to Ward's volume. After its appearance in the *Saturday Press*, Twain's story became so popular that it was reprinted across the country. In the letter to his mother mentioned above, Twain included a clipping from the San Francisco *Alta California*, which was then recognized as San Francisco's "establishment paper." The clipping described the effect "The Jumping Frog" was having on the literary world of New York: "Mark Twain's story in the *Saturday Press* of November 18 . . . has set New York in a roar, and he may be said to have made his mark. . . . The papers are copying it far and near. It is voted the best thing of the day. Cannot the *Californian* afford to keep Mark all to itself? It should not let him scintillate so widely without first being filtered through the California press." In his letter home, Twain went on to deny the intrinsic value of the story that was making him a celebrity on the Atlantic Coast as well as on the Pacific: "To think that after writing many an article a man might be excused for thinking tolerably good, those New York people should single out a villainous back-woods sketch to compliment me on!"

The letter also contained some enthusiastic praise of Bret Harte. "Though I am generally placed at the head of my breed of scribblers in this part of the country, the place properly belongs to Bret Harte, though he denies it, along with the rest." The clouds of dissension that were to obscure the Twain/Harte friendship had not yet descended, and at the time "The Jumping Frog" was taking the country by storm, the two writers were still sharing the limelight in what passed for peaceable coexistence.

It isn't hard to understand why Clemens was so incensed at the East Coast folks who were praising him for the frog story. He was always uncomfortable in the role of "Wild Humorist of the Pacific Slope," and the frog story played up that role almost more than anything else he had ever written. Yet it was the only thing he had ever written that had appeared in a New York magazine. Although Twain was sorry that his first appearance before a national audience had to be of such slight substance, the Mother Lode amphibian was destined to serve its purpose nonetheless. As the plaudits continued to roll in for his "villainous back-woods sketch," Twain began at last to realize that California was becoming his springboard to a larger success. Ironically, this sketch, which he had first heard in a Mother Lode tavern, would not only elevate Twain to the ranks of the exalted, but would also guarantee San Francisco and California their respectives niches in the literary hall of fame.

7
"OUR FELLOW SAVAGES OF THE SANDWICH ISLANDS"

DESPITE HIS LITERARY

success, all was not well with Mark Twain in the early months of 1866. The fact that his reputation as a writer was growing by leaps and bounds seemed to mean little to him. Perhaps the feeling that he was the most noteworthy literary figure in what was, after all, a cultural backwater made him place a lesser value on his success than he should have; or perhaps his riotous style of living was taking its toll (he had recently been jailed overnight for public drunkenness). In January or February of that year, Twain tried to commit suicide by putting a loaded pistol to his head. He sat there for some minutes, trying to summon the courage to pull the trigger, but he was unable to do it. Years later he looked back on the incident: "Many times I have been sorry I did not succeed, but I was never ashamed of having tried."

It was also at this time that the unpleasantness between Twain and his old enemy, "Fitz Smythe," reached a shrill crescendo. Writing in the Nevada Gold Hill *News* under the name "Amigo," Evans hinted that he knew things about Twain's private life that would ruin his reputation forever. For instance, said "Amigo," the "Bohemian from the sage-brush" had "lost $40 in the house of a lady, under peculiar circumstances." Clemens, he went on, "had also lost his watch in the aforementioned establishment," though "he thought the police had stolen it on the night previous, having been oblivious to the fact that his friend had taken it from him early in the evening, in order to save him from loss." Finally, "Amigo" insinuated, Twain "probably had a venereal disease." Evans seemed especially interested in Twain's medical history, for in another nasty attack in the Gold Hill *News* a couple of weeks later, he made the following observation:

I understand that [Mark Twain] . . . is disgusted with San Francisco. Well, my boy, the disgust is mutual, and I don't wonder that he wants to leave. . . . He has been a little out of health of late and is now endeavoring to get a chance to go to Honolulu, where he expects to get rid of one disease by catching another; the last being more severe for the time being, but more readily yielding to medical treatment. . . . If he goes he will be sadly missed by the police, but then they can stand it.

Twain was most definitely interested in getting out of San Francisco at that time. Hoping to assuage his growing restlessness, he had already been to Sacramento to report on that city for the *Enterprise*. He arrived there from San Francisco in early February at 3 A.M. one morning "in company with several other disreputable characters," he wrote, "on board the good steamer *Antelope*, Captain Poole, commander."

True to character, Twain's first impression of the state capital was that it was "the City of Saloons." "I know I am departing from usage in calling Sacramento the City of Saloons instead of the City of the Plains," he apologized in his first article, "but I have my justification — I have not found any plains here, yet, but I have been in most of the saloons, and there are a good many of them. You can shut your eyes and march into the first door you come to and call for a drink, and the chances are that you will get it."

Then Twain remembered that he was supposed to be describing some of the other things in Sacramento, so he included a "Brief Climate Paragraph": "This is the mildest, balmiest, pleasantest climate one can imagine. The evenings are especially delightful — neither too warm nor too cold. I wonder if it is always so?"

Following this obligatory attention to detail, he returned to subjects closer to his heart, such as relations with the proprietor of his hotel—"a large, fine-looking man, with a chest which must have made him a most powerful man before it slid down." He and Clemens had a number of disagreements, and in his Sacramento article entitled "I Try To Out 'Sass' The Landlord—And Fail," Twain recorded the following exchange of pleasantries between them:

"Old Smarty from Mud Springs, I apprehend," Twain hissed within the innkeeper's hearing.

"Young Lunar Caustic from San Francisco, no doubt," the proprietor snarled back.

The people of Sacramento, much to their credit, seemed to appreciate Twain's various musings about their fair city as much as did Clemens's readers in Virginia City and San Francisco. This fact was taken due notice of by the publishers of the Sacramento *Union*, James Anthony and Paul Morrill. When Twain had introduced himself to them and they had judged him to be reasonably reliable, he laid a proposal before them, to which he had given much thought. ("Amigo" had referred to this plan of Twain's in his nasty diatribe.) Some months previously, Twain had been invited to join a select group of passengers on the maiden voyage of the *Ajax*, which had been built for the rapidly growing trade between the United States and the Sandwich (later Hawaiian) Islands. Twain had been unable to go on that first trip, because he had been locked into a dull routine, sending the *Enterprise* daily letters from San Francisco.

Now, however, Twain explained to the publishers of the Sacramento *Union*, the good ship *Ajax* was back in San Francisco and was due soon to make another voyage to the islands. He asked Anthony and Morrill if they would consider paying his fare to the islands on board the *Ajax* in exchange for a series of articles for their paper. He argued (somewhat truthfully) that the Sandwich Islands' sugar industry was beginning to mean a great deal to California's economy and was thus newsworthy. Furthermore, the islands' scenery and the customs of the natives would make fascinating reading for the *Union's* readers, he promised. Twain's salesmanship was generally successful, and this time was no exception, for Anthony and Morrill, for reasons best known to themselves, acquiesced to Twain's proposal. It certainly wasn't going to do the *Union* any harm to have the man who was rapidly becoming California's most celebrated writer serving as their Sandwich Islands correspondent, and it wasn't even that expensive to hire his services.

When Twain received the good news, all his ennui and depression vanished immediately, leaving only a little alcoholic vapor behind. He became so carried away with the notion of traveling, in fact, that he threw himself into an orgy of further travel planning. He figured that once he was back from the islands, he would head straight across the continental United States: up the Columbia River, through Montana, and down the Missouri River to his boyhood home. It didn't matter to him whether or not he would ever complete the ambitous trip he had outlined for himself—it was the *idea* of traveling that had caught his fancy at the moment.

On March 7, 1866, he hung over the rail of the *Ajax* as she steamed out of San Francisco harbor, leaning into the crisp, refreshing wind that whipped the wavelets of the Golden Gate into stiff white peaks and caused his bushy red hair to fly wildly about his face. Bret Harte's initial impression of Clemens had been that he was a man "whose general manner was one of supreme indifference to surroundings and circumstances," but nothing could have been further from the truth. Twain was a natural travel writer. Few others would ever be able to equal his sharp eye for detail and the amazing sense of place he possessed after spending only a few hours in a new environment. At the moment, on board the *Ajax*, he was positively glorifying in the notion that he was heading somewhere wild and unknown. Years later, after crisscrossing the globe dozens of times, Twain would lose his appetite for new places, for they would no longer be new to him. But in 1866, as he leaned over the rail of the *Ajax*, travel was a completely fresh experience for him, and he felt as if all the cobwebs of his previous life were blowing away.

He arrived in Honolulu on March 18. From then until he left the Sandwich Islands the following July, he claimed to have enjoyed "half a year's luxurious vagrancy in the islands." This was, of course, one of his typical "stretchers"; his visit lasted only four and a half months, and those months were not exactly frittered away in idleness. During that period, he sent back twenty-five articles to the *Union* which ranged in length from 1,800 to 3,500 words. For each of these, he was paid twenty dollars.

In order to pack the articles full of information, Twain "ransacked the islands, the cataracts and the volcanoes completely." He did this by traveling around the islands on horseback and on foot, passing from island to island on intraisland packets like the wretched

Boomerang. The *Boomerang's* route lay between Honolulu and the "big island" of Hawaii, a trip of one hundred and fifty miles. She was a cramped, dingy, derelict craft with minuscule cabins for the first-class passengers such as Twain. In *Roughing It* Twain recalled his first night out aboard the *Boomerang*, lying in a bunk that resembled a coffin and pestered half to death by overly sociable rats, enormous cockroaches with "long quivering antennae and fiery, malignant eyes," and acrobatic fleas who "were throwing double somersaults about my person in the wildest disorder, and taking a bite every time they struck."

The trip aboard the *Boomerang* was illustrative of the rugged conditions of life Twain found in the islands—conditions that, surprisingly, he endured bravely and even uncomplainingly. The novelty of life in the islands was apparently enough to keep his mind off the discomforts he suffered, although he generally preferred luxury over "roughing it."

He observed the islands' native population at some length and with the greatest of interest, just as he had surveyed local Indian tribes in California and Nevada. In Washoe, he had speculated about the supposedly romantic origins of the Indian name "Tahoe," finally explaining that the name meant nothing more exalted than "grasshopper soup," that perennial favorite of the Paiute Indians. Now, in his articles from the islands, Twain had a great deal to say about the islands' natives, or "Kanakas" as they were called. One thing Twain observed was that due to the warm climate of the islands, the Kanakas wore very little clothing. The nineteenth century got to tugging at him a little, reminding him that only savages don't have an inborn sense of modesty, but Twain's basic nature found the seminudity of the Kanakas to be a charming and (in view of the climate) a logical thing.

His opinion may have changed as a result of an interlude in Honolulu. One afternoon, as he was sitting on the beach, he encountered a group of lovely young island women. They came running toward him down the white stretch of sand, then threw off their scanty clothing and dashed past him, diving into the sparkling surf. Twain wrote about the incident in his correspondence for the *Union*, joking that he had been obliged to remain on the beach guarding their clothes until they finally came out of the water. On other occasions, he admitted to being enchanted by the complete lack of self-consciousness evinced by the island women in their natural state; he found their "rounded forms, inclining to the voluptuous" wondrous to behold. Whenever he felt guilty about praising the Kanakas too much, he tried to modify his praise by adding such negative observations as the fact that the Kanaka population were inveterate liars; they would, said Twain, "lie for a dollar when they could get a dollar and a half for telling the truth." Mostly, however, he found the islands' natives as interesting as any group of uncivilized heathens could be.

TWAIN SOON DISCOVERED

that his reputation as the most popular writer in San Francisco had preceded him to the islands; everywhere he went, he found a hearty welcome from his fellow Americans. In the cool, shady, stately homes where he stayed, on plantations as well as in the islands' few cities, he found the company exceedingly cordial. The relaxed pace of life enjoyed by the island dwellers appeared to him to be a tonic for stress as well as a promoter of tranquility and contentment. In his notebook, he observed that he saw "no careworn or eager, anxious faces in this land of happy contentment. God, what a contrast with California and the Washoe!" And, "They *live* in the Sandwich Islands – no rush, no worry – merchant goes down to his store like a gentleman at nine – goes home at four and *thinks no more* of business till next day. Damned San F. style of wearing out life."

Perhaps he was unaware of it, but his view of the islands was hardly a complete one. The Sandwich Islands expedition occurred at a point in Twain's life when he had not yet become antiimperialistic, as he would in later years. In fact, as he talked with the American plantation owners, he became firmly convinced that the United States should annex the Sandwich Islands in order to reap the benefits of the islands' bountiful sugar and coffee crops and other resources. Although he had taken the side of the Chinese immigrant workers in San Francisco, he seemed to see no contradiciton between his earlier and present opinions when he viewed the Chinese laborers who toiled in the sugar cane fields as a fine source of cheap, hard-working manpower that made the Hawaiian sugar industry all the more promising for the United States.

Despite his perennial disenchantment with organized religion, Twain also had nothing especially scathing to say about the American missionaries who had come to the islands in the earlier part of the century, and who were continuing their self-appointed task of "civilizing" the Kanakas as only they knew how. Later, Twain would change his attitude about the missionaries—in relatively short order, as a matter of fact—but during his stay in the islands he only praised them for eradicating native superstition, without stopping to think what they had replaced that superstition *with*.

The Volcano of Kilauea

was still active during Twain's sojourn in the islands, and he had heard so much about it that he determined to get as close to its explosive central crater as possible. With an equally reckless fellow named Marlette, who was familiar with the multifarious nooks and crannies of the mammoth fire mountain, Twain walked directly across the floor of the volcano's crater by night, dashing lightly over sheets of fiery lava that flowed around his feet, and leaping across wide crevices from which the molten fire trapped inside emitted a baleful red glow.

At one point, his guide shouted for him to stop. "I never stopped quicker in my life," wrote Twain in *Roughing It*. "I asked what the matter was. He said we were out of the path. He said we must not go on until we found it again, for we were surrounded with beds of rotten lava, through which we could easily break and plunge down 1,000 feet. I thought 800 would answer for me, and was about to say so, when Marlette partly proved his statement, crushing through and disappearing to his arm-pits."

Marlette got out all right, and the two explorers proceeded to spend the rest of the night gazing down into the hellish depths of the red-hot crater. This was an experience that Twain relished intensely and that he remembered vividly for the rest of his life, often retelling it in such a way that it struck awe and wonder into the hearts of visitors. The idea of risking his neck to peer into the very depths of a live and malevolent volcano was a notion that thrilled Twain to the depths of his soul.

At the End of June

he returned to Honolulu from his wanderings, intending to rest for a while and nurse the saddle boils he had accumulated during his travels on horseback around the islands. He was lying in bed in his hotel room in Honolulu when he received a message from some very august personages indeed, saying that they were going to pay him a call at his hotel the next morning.

Twain was shaken up considerably at this news, for the party was headed up by His Excellency Anson Burlingame, who had just arrived on the *Ajax* from San Francisco en route to a diplomatic post as American minister to China. There were also some other American diplomats who were traveling to China with Burlingame — Generals Van Valkenberg and Rumsey, respectively, as well as Burlingame's eighteen-year-old son, Edward. Clemens was no stranger to the workings of politics, nor was he particularly sentimental when it came to the bloated aristocrats of political pomp. Nonetheless, after hearing through channels in Honolulu that Burlingame's son Edward was a big fan of "The Jumping Frog" and wanted very much to meet its author, he positively beamed. However, he realized that, saddle boils or no saddle boils, it would be quite unseemly to oblige such an exalted group to call on him in his hotel room, so the next morning he dragged himself painfully out of bed, applied a pair of pants as gingerly as he could over the affected area, and drove with all haste to the house belonging to the American minister to the Sandwich Islands, where Burlingame and company were quartered.

His visit was an unqualified success, for he was careful to pull out all the stops and make himself thoroughly agreeable and amusing, and the diplomats found his charm irresistible. For his part, Twain was considerably impressed by Anson Burlingame, and remained so throughout his life. Burlingame gave him a piece of advice that the Sagebrush Bohemian saw fit to take to heart, for better or for worse: "You have great ability; I believe you have genius. What you need now is the refinement of association. Seek companionship among men of superior intellect and character. Refine yourself and your work. Never affiliate with inferiors; always climb."

Burlingame did Twain a far greater favor by helping him get a "scoop" on a very important story. A large vessel, the *Hornet*, had left New York some weeks earlier and had caught fire out in the middle of the ocean, leaving fifteen survivors to battle the rolling deep for a whole month in a tiny lifeboat with only ten days' rations of food and water. Eleven of these human relics had arrived in Honolulu on June 21, and Twain immediately realized that it would be an incredible scoop if he could somehow interview these sufferers for the *Union*. He was the only correspondent for any American paper then in the islands. But, because he had overtaxed himself physically, his health had taken a turn for the worse, and he was under doctor's orders to get in bed and stay there. The question uppermost in his mind was, how could he drag himself to the hospital in Honolulu where the survivors were, and interview them?

It was Anson Burlingame to the rescue. Burlingame, with military decisiveness, ascertained the situation at once, and without further ado bore the prostrate Clemens to the hospital on a stretcher, then proceeded to interview the survivors himself while Twain propped himself up on his elbow and took notes. That night Twain wrote feverishly and finished his article just in time to heave it aboard the California-bound steamer as it was leaving Honolulu pier the next morning. The "scoop" on the *Hornet* disaster ran in three columns on the front page of the *Union*, and was the first (and fullest) story of the tragedy to appear in any American newspaper.

Twain had fully recovered by early July, and he took ship for San Francisco on July 19 on the vessel *Smyrniote*. He spent most of the voyage home talking with the captain of the ill-fated *Hornet* as well with some of the other survivors, who were headed for San Francisco. He also copied a number of passages from their assorted diaries. It was his intention to write an article about the disaster for a New York magazine—thinking, no doubt, of the further inroads this might make on the East Coast literary Parnassus.

On the voyage home, he otherwise employed himself by leading the ship's choir during Sunday services. "I hope they will have a better opinion of our music in heaven than I have down here," he reflected in his journal. "If they don't a thunderbolt will knock this vessel endways." The heavens did make a sort of gesture in his direction, however; he saw another moonlit rainbow on the night of July 27, and once again looked upon it as representing an auspicious future.

However, once he arrived in San Francisco and was faced with the same old grind he thought he had left behind, all his elation rapidly dissolved, and he suffered the remorse that affects every vacationer on returning home. "God help me, I wish I were at sea again!" he confided to his journal.

In Sacramento, the last of his Sandwich Islands articles were running in the *Union* and they were being very well received by the public. Twain accordingly made another trip to the "City of Saloons" to report on the California State Fair for the *Union* – or rather, on the horse races that were one of the fair's biggest attractions. He may have done so as a favor to the *Union's* James Anthony, for it was rather routine work and in some ways even reminiscent of the ig-nominious drudgery he had suffered as the *Call's* lokulitems. But the favor ultimately paid off handsomely, if in a roundabout way, for when the time came for the settling of accounts between Twain and Anthony for the *Hornet* disaster scoop, the *Union's* proprietor was extremely generous. "How much do you think it ought to be, Mark?" Anthony asked Twain.

"Oh, I'm a modest man; I don't want the whole *Union* office," replied Twain with mock diffidence. "Call it $100 a column."

Anthony and Paul Morrill laughed, but they made out a pay-ment order for the amount Twain specified. Twain took it down to the paper's cashier, who could only look at the amount apoplectically. "The cashier didn't faint," Twain remembered, "but he came rather near it. He sent for the proprietors, and they only laughed, in their jolly fashion, and said it was a robbery, but 'no matter, pay it.'" It was little wonder that Twain recalled them fondly as "the best men that ever owned a newspaper."

8
THE TROUBLE
BEGINS
AT EIGHT

BACK IN SAN FRANCISCO,

Twain was forced once again to think of ways to earn some money. This, of course, meant a return to the old grind of journalism. Then, too, after the luxurious greenery of the Sandwich Islands, San Francisco seemed barren and dreary to Twain. "San Francisco, a truly fascinating city to live in, is stately and handsome at a fair distance, but close at hand one notes that the architecture is mostly old-fashioned, many streets are made up of decaying, smoke-grimed, wooden houses, and the barren sand-hills towards the outskirts obtrude themselves too prominently." This was how he was later to describe the city in *Roughing It*, and it is a fair assumption that it reflected his feelings about San Francisco at the time he returned from the islands.

Another thing that was bothering him was the fact that, despite the success of "The Jumping Frog," he didn't seem to have set his feet on any sure path to continuing literary success. He had written up the *Hornet* disaster for *Harper's* magazine in New York, and the article had been accepted and published, but much to Twain's dismay, the article had run under the byline "Mark Swain" thanks to some careless typesetter. All Twain's hopes of achieving recognition on the East Coast as a serious writer were dashed to the ground by this one seemingly insignificant error, for of course no one had any idea who "Mark Swain" was. It was one of those maddening occurrences that were to make such great material for his subsequent books and essays, but at the moment it happened, he felt far from philosophical about it.

Despite his depression at being back in the grimy city and forced once again to scramble for his bread and butter, Twain was formulating all sorts of plans for future projects. He had an idea for a series of articles in *Harper's*, or in any national magazine, in which he would enlarge on his Sacramento *Union* letters from the Sandwich Islands. Such a series, he reasoned, could prove popular enough in the long run to enable him to wangle a book contract—and an advance—to further enlarge on the articles. Travel books were extremely welcome to readers in an age when the only long-distance travel was accomplished by the slow and costly steamboat. As a matter of fact, Twain himself was an inveterate reader of travel books. He had turned to them for facts and figures while writing his Sandwich Islands articles, but he also enjoyed perusing them for sheer entertainment. He was well aware of the marketability of such books, for he knew a number of northern California–based authors who, in essence, were being paid to travel—that is, they received sizable sums for books about their peregrinations. One of these authors was J. Ross Browne, a personal friend of Twain's whose travel books had enabled him to build a sumptuous and exotic home in what would today be considered a part of Berkeley. (Later, Browne would jocularly accuse Twain of "borrowing" from his travel books, although whether there was any truth to this or not is a matter open to conjecture.)

Another money-making idea that Twain was mulling over was one that both terrified and titillated him—the idea of giving a public lecture about the Sandwich Islands. Travel lectures were even more popular than travel books and could bring in a fair amount of revenue for lecturers, especially if the lecturers were willing to undertake a lecturing tour. In view of his literary reputation on the Pacific Coast, Twain felt that he would have no trouble filling halls in San Francisco, Sacramento, and Washoe. The problem was that he had some rather serious doubts about his ability to speak before large groups of people—especially paying customers. He had never really done it before, although he was no stranger to public speaking done for love rather than money. Back in Nevada in 1863, for instance, when he had been covering the meeting of that year's Territorial Legislature, he had been elected president of the "Third House." The Third House was a mock legislature convened for the amusement of political observers. Its main function was to satirize and parody the current politicians and issues facing the regular legislature. It "elected" its own officers, who went out of their way to make caricature of the Territorial Legislature's political hacks—a situation tailor-made for Twain, with his eagle eye for human folly and bombast. In his elevated position as president of the Third House, he had stood before the "legislature" aping the various irritating little foibles of the regular legislature's members, down to the very last "I, uh . . . I, uh" and coat-button fumbling. The other "members" of the Third House, as well as the large public audience that gathered to witness the festivities, were thoroughly delighted with this performance of Twain's, and as a result his fame as a stand-up comic was sung all over the Territory.

Twain was also almost a legend in Washoe and San Francisco for his ability to keep saloon and tavern audiences hanging on his every word. Even in his early writings, he showed himself to be a master of colloquial conversation rather than the flowery "literary" style that was then in vogue. He was fully aware of the artistry involved in telling a story effectively—but that was hardly the same thing as delivering an informative lecture to a stiff and starchy audience who had paid for the privilege of hearing him.

Like the former steamboat pilot he was, Twain thus decided to "test the water" before he attempted to navigate in it. First he wrote out a rough draft of his proposed lecture and showed it to some friends whose opinions he valued. Unfortunately, he didn't receive much encouragement from them. A reporter he knew, for instance, looked over the lecture and expressed the fear that Twain might not be able to talk as well as he could write. Bret Harte and Charles Stoddard, fellow Bohemians whose opinions Twain practically took for gospel in those days, expressed similar doubts. At such discouraging reactions, Twain's spirits sank, but he didn't give up— just yet. He continued to show his manuscript around, and he finally found somebody to support his proposed lecturing career. It was a newspaper editor—some say Colonel John McComb of the *Alta*, others say the proprietor of the *Call*, George Barnes, with whom Twain had remained on good terms following his dismissal from that paper. At any rate, this editor, whoever he was, read Twain's proposed lecture, then wrung Twain's sweaty hand with vigor and bellowed, "Do it, by all means! It will be a grand success, I know it! Take the largest house in town, and charge a dollar a ticket!"

A dollar a ticket! Twain felt slightly ill at the thought of asking people to pay so bloated and grandiose a sum merely to hear him drawl his way through descriptions of heathens and volcanoes. Still, charging a dollar a ticket was so audacious that it was bound to attract a considerable number of curiosity seekers, whether Twain's actual career as a lecturer turned out to be stillborn or not. So he proceeded over to Maguire's Opera House on Pine Street, the newest and fanciest theater in San Francisco. Tom Maguire, its owner, had owned the opera house in Virginia City and was an old acquaintance of Twain's, and he agreed to let the tyro speaker have his establishment for half the usual rate — only fifty dollars a night.

On September 27, 1866, the people of San Francisco discovered that the city had been liberally plastered with the following announcement:

MAGUIRE'S ACADEMY OF MUSIC
PINE STREET, NEAR MONTGOMERY

THE SANDWICH ISLANDS

MARK TWAIN
(HONOLULU CORRESPONDENT OF THE SACRAMENTO UNION)
WILL DELIVER A

LECTURE ON THE SANDWICH ISLANDS
AT THE ACADEMY OF MUSIC
ON TUESDAY EVENING, OCT. 2d
(1866)

In which passing mention will be made of Harris, Bishop Staley, the American missionaries, etc., and the absurd customs and characteristics of the natives duly discussed and described. The great volcano of Kilauea will also receive proper attention.

A SPLENDID ORCHESTRA
is in town, but *has not* been engaged
ALSO
A DEN OF FEROCIOUS WILD BEASTS
will be on exhibition in the next block

MAGNIFICENT FIREWORKS
were in contemplation for this occasion, but the idea has been abandoned

A GRAND TORCHLIGHT PROCESSION
may be expected; in fact, the public are privileged to expect whatever they please.

Dress Circle, $1.00   Family Circle, 50¢

Doors open at 7 o'clock   The Trouble to begin at 8 o'clock

This same advertisement assaulted the eyes of San Francisco's citizens from the pages of several newspapers. Like the bogus "Duke" in *Huckleberry Finn*, Twain knew enough about lurid advertising to understand what would "fetch them."

Now, however, he proceeded to sweat. First he looked over his lecture again in the harsh, cold light of reality, and it seemed to him that nothing he had ever clapped eyes on was as tiresome, tedious, and utterly bereft of humor. He felt so disheartened, in fact, that he began to regret that he couldn't just "bring a coffin on the stage and turn the whole thing into a funeral."

Expecting the absolute worst, he decided to stagger his odds as best as he could. He rushed to three old drinking companions, "giants in stature, cordial by nature, and stormy-voiced," and asked if they would serve as "plants" in the audience on the fateful (or, Clemens though morosely, the fatal) night. "This thing is going to be a failure," Twain observed to them melodramatically. "The jokes in it are so dim that nobody will ever see them; I would like to have you sit in the parquette, and help me through."

The three good fellows agreed wholeheartedly to laugh uproariously at even the most slender excuse for a joke. Next Twain sought out the wife of "a popular citizen," and explained to her, as he had to his three friends, that he feared his lecture was going to need all the help it could get; then he asked if she and her husband would sit in the box next to the left of the stage. Whenever he had thrown out the punchline of an especially obscure joke, he explained, he would turn toward her and smile, as a signal. Then she shouldn't "wait to investigate, but *respond!*"

Finally, a few days before the lecture, Twain happened to stumble across a random wino on the street who was "beaming with smiles and good nature," as befitted his vaporous state. He recognized Twain and approached him with a view to panhandling a free ticket to the lecture. At first Twain pretended to be doubtful. "Is your laugh hung on a hair-trigger?" he demanded. "That is, is it critical, or can you get it off easy?"

Twain's "drawling infirmity of speech" so tickled the derelict that he at once emitted a specimen of laughter that struck Twain as just about the article he wanted, and he promptly bestowed a "comp" on the fellow and instructed him to sit in the second dress circle, thereby "dividing the house." Clemens additionally give him minute instructions on how he might detect indistinct jokes, then left the wino chuckling over the downright novelty of the whole notion.

TWAIN CLAIMED LATER

he ate nothing for three days before the horrible event – he only suffered. At four in the afternoon on the day of the lecture, he crept down to the box office at Maguire's; that was the time when the tickets for the evening's performance went on sale. Much to his horror, he found that the ticket office was locked up and the ticket seller had gone home! "No sales," he said to himself, and added bitterly, "I might have known it!" Desperately, he contemplated an array of last-minute ruses and dodges to get him out of the public humiliation he was sure the lecture would be – everything from faked illness to outright flight, and maybe even another shot at suicide. But he also knew that he had to go through with it, even if it killed him.

At six that evening, he approached the opera house by way of a back street and sneaked in through the stage door. The auditorium was empty, dark, and resoundingly silent. For a brief moment Twain stood on the stage, staring dully out at the rows upon rows of empty seats. Then he turned and went back into the wings, where for an hour and a half he gave himself up to "the horrors," wholly unconscious of everything else.

"Then," he recalled in *Roughing It*, "I heard a murmur. It rose higher and higher, and ended in a crash, mingled with cheers. . . . There was a pause, and then another; presently came a third, and before I well knew what I was about, I was in the middle of the stage, staring at a sea of faces, bewildered by the fierce glare of the lights, and quaking in every limb with a terror that seemed like to take my life away. The house was full, aisles and all!"

The trouble had begun at eight, as promised in Twain's advertising.

Twain's version of that first lecture, full as it is of the mingled sense of drama and absurdity that characterize his style of narration, has more than one gaping hole in it. For one thing, it is highly unlikely that he would have been overly worried about no one showing up to hear him lecture. His several years as a popular writer, both in Washoe and in California, not to mention the recent fame of "The Jumping Frog," made his lecturing debut an event of considerable importance around town. Moreover, San Francisco's various newspapers had all commented upon Twain's lecture at a point when it was practically still a gleam in its perpetrator's eagle eye. The *Call*, for instance, had opined, "We have no doubt that the house will be crowded," and "We may rest assured that the lecture will be a good one." The *Evening Bulletin* had also praised the event in advance: "Those who wish to get seats will do well to go early, for the indications of a grand rush are unmistakable." From this end of time it is not so hard to take Twain's version of his first lecture at face value, for there is something undeniably noble about the notion of triumph snatched from the jaws of oblivion; but the estimated house count that night numbered between 1,500 and 2,000 fashionably dressed, socially prominent San Franciscans. Maguire's Opera House was quite literally packed to the rafters, with a large number of male attendees being forced to stand against the wall in the back.

That night, Twain opened his remarks with an eloquent apology for the absence of the orchestra he had promised in his advertisements. He went on to explain that he had gone so far as to hire the services of "a performer on a gorgeous trombone," but had discovered that that unreasonable individual had required half a dozen others to "help him." Since he had hired that trombonist to work, Twain told the audience, he had been obliged to let the fellow go promptly upon hearing such nonsense.

This was just the first of a string of jokes that Twain unreeled at his listeners, and they responded with peals of hearty laughter. Finally, when he judged that the climate was appropriate, Twain commenced the "meat and potatoes" part of the evening—the portion pertaining to the Sandwich Islands. He delineated the virtues of the Kanakas at some length, and touched on their vices with good-natured humor. He gave pertinent data on the islands' climate, vegetation, geography, history, traditions, superstitions, religion, politics, government, royalty, manners, and customs—all of which information was imparted in a humorous and thoroughly painless fashion. During the course of the lecture, he also recommended that the United States annex the islands to the mainland, and enthused about all the economic advantages the islands would offer, once they were under the protection of the U.S. flag. As mentioned earlier, this gung-ho imperialism was an early philosophy of his; later, he

SEVERE CASE OF STAGE-FRIGHT.

would state flatly that he was "opposed to having the eagle put its talons on any other land."

Twain also let the islands' meddlesome missionaries off rather lightly during his first lecture, praising them for having rid the Kanakas of superstition and elevating the natives to a peaceful, if still largely uncivilized, condition. Most of the members of the audience knew that Twain attended San Francisco's Presbyterian church on occasion, and that he thoroughly enjoyed the company of ministers, so such statements did not strike them as contradicting his basically atheistic beliefs. (Twain eventually began billing his Sandwich Islands lecture as "Our Fellow Savages of the Sandwich Islands," but that was not until a little later.)

The high point of the evening, however, was Twain's lofty and eloquent description of the volcano, Mt. Kilauea – a description that reportedly had the audience's more susceptible members dabbing surreptitiously at their eyes with their handkerchiefs. In his characteristic drawl, Twain let roll off his tongue the most vivid description of an erupting volcano that had ever roused an audience to a standing ovation:

When the volcano of Kilauea broke through a few years ago, lava flowed out of it for twenty days and twenty nights, and made a stream forty miles in length, till it reached the sea, tearing up forests in its awful fiery path, swallowing up huts, destroying all vegetation, rioting through shady dells and sinuous canyons. Amid this carnival of destruction, majestic columns of smoke ascended and formed a cloudy, murky pall overhead. Sheets of green, blue, lambent flames were shot upward, and pierced the vast gloom, making all sublimely grand.

After Twain concluded his lecture, which lasted an hour and a half (an unheard-of length for such an event), the audience simply refused to let him off the stage. When he excused himself and walked off into the wings, the crowd stood up and persistently applauded, cheered, and stamped until it seemed as though the roof would cave in. At this unanimous command, Twain shuffled back onstage again, looking around with a puzzled expression as if he couldn't understand what all the commotion was about. Then, pressed by the audience to say something further, he apologized to everyone for having "inflicted" his lecture on them in the first place. He explained that he was writing a book about the islands and said that he needed money to get it published. After receiving another thunderous round of applause that rivaled an erupting Kilauea for sheer number of decibels, Twain bowed once again and left the stage.

THE NEXT DAY ALL THE

San Francisco papers were full of Clemens's triumph. The *Evening Bulletin* trumpeted that "as a humorous writer Mark Twain stands in the foremost rank, while his effort of last evening affords reason for the belief that he can establish an equal reputation as a humorous and original lecturer." The *Dramatic Chronicle*, for which Twain had begun to write following his dismissal from the *Call*, declared that his lecture "may be pronounced one of the greatest successes of the season."

Only Prentice Mulford, writing in the *Golden Era*, felt obliged to be a little contrary. Mulford had, among other things, taken a largely unsuccessful crack at public lecturing in California's mining towns, and he now warned Twain about attempting a lecture career. "I shall venture on the terrible risk of criticizing Mark Twain," he said in his critique of the lecture. "It is a perilous undertaking. He wields a pen mightily in ridicule and sarcasm, and woe unto him who provokes his displeasure." Mulford then went on to tease Twain gently: "Indeed it is not right that in one person should be combined so many species of talent. It is enough that (Twain) is a good writer. Let the gifts be distributed equally." Like some of the other reviewers, Mulford noted that Twain's speaking voice could have been louder at times, a fault evidenced by many people new to the lecture platform. Mulford concluded his review by cautioning Twain on the many pitfalls that awaited a lecturer touring mining camps and other remote outposts of civilization.

All those who reviewed Twain's lecture were unanimous on one point: as a humorous lecturer, Twain was far superior to his old friend Artemus Ward. Mulford pointed out, "Mark's humor is his own, while much of Ward's is begged and borrowed." In his Washoe days, Twain had paid careful attention to Ward's platform mannerisms, and while no one could accuse him of actually stealing from Ward, it was plain that he had made many valuable mental notes about what went over well with Ward's audiences; but there all similarities ended, for Twain used his own powerful personality to hold things together.

It was obvious to everyone that Twain's personal style had contributed vitally to the remarkable success of his first lecture. With considerable shrewdness, he had played up his lack of experience as a public lecturer. On the platform, his face had worn an anxious, worried expression; his delivery was slow and almost pained, framed in his own inimitable drawl, with the words coming so slowly that one Washoe newspaper typesetter was later to observe that it sounded as though there was "a three-em quad" between each one. Then, too, there was something strangely touching (if a trifle stagey) about Twain's tendency to appear thunderstruck whenever he scored a humorous hit with the audience, as though he couldn't believe his own success.

Most unusually for a lecturer at that time, Twain eschewed the customary flights of pompous oratory in favor of a strictly conversational style of patter. He used the same approach in his writing, it is true, but because he was writing primarily in newspapers, his colloquial approach was far less noticeable. The critics were sharply divided when it came to Twain's penchant for lacing his lecture with liberal doses of slang. Bret Harte complained that Twain's only fault as a lecturer was too much "crudeness and coarseness," and his sentiments were echoed by other reviewers, but Twain's audience didn't seem to object too strenuously; apparently Clemens knew exactly how far he could go without sending the gentler members of his audience fleeing up the aisle with their hands over their ears.

Nonetheless, none of the writers who reviewed Twain's first public lecture really hit on the fundamental reason for his success both in writing and in public speaking. This was simply that Clemens, despite considerable personal eccentricity, was able to communicate a basically human quality that few people could resist. At the root of his humor was a thorough understanding of human nature, with all its capacity for self-delusion, dishonesty, folly — and nobility. It was easy for Twain's audience to identify with him when he stood, apparently terrified, behind the podium; their hearts went out to him as he sweated and drawled his way through what was actually an extremely eloquent speech. Perhaps this wasn't the first time anyone had combined pathos and humor with eloquence, but when Twain did so, any previous practitioners of that art were instantly forgotten. It was a tribute to his own originality and daring that his lecture career had gotten off to such a brilliant start; but his first audience at Maguire's Opera House had helped some too. If they hadn't been as enthusiastic in their reception of that lecture, Twain would never have been launched on the lecturing career that was to last for the remainder of his life.

9
FAREWELL
TO THE
BARBARY
COAST

WHEN TWAIN COUNTED UP

the proceeds from his lecture, he was no doubt impressed with his own business acumen. The gross came to $1,200; after paying for the advertising and giving Tom Maguire fifty dollars for the rental of the Opera House, Twain still had $400 left in his pocket – untold riches, considering that the day before had had been almost flat broke.

As his reputation as a lecturer began to spread via newspapers all over the Pacific Coast, the most logical thing seemed to be for Twain to undertake a lecture tour of California and Nevada. He was later to joke that after his first lecture tour was successful, he acquired a back-up profession and never had to work for a living again in his life. While this was only partly true, lecturing was clearly the thing for him to be doing at that time.

One of the first things that he did was to appoint a gentleman named Denis McCarthy as his business manager. McCarthy wasn't really a gentleman. However, he happened to be in San Francisco at that time with no fixed address and no permanent employment, and Twain thus considered him an ideal business manager for an itinerant lecturer. According to legend, McCarthy had been sitting in the office of the *Territorial Enterprise* on the day in 1862 when the dusty and demented Samuel Clemens had wandered in from his 130-mile hike, looking for employment. That fact alone endeared McCarthy to Twain; besides, in Washoe McCarthy had also been a boon companion of Clemens's during drinking sprees and other similar recreations, and had even assisted Twain, Dan De Quille, and Joe Goodman during the notorious three weeks when Artemus Ward had been in Nevada and had been so royally entertained by the *Enterprise* staff.

With this important business decision made, Twain laid out his itinerary, after a fashion. He and McCarthy decided to make Sacramento their first stop. The two partners accordingly took passage on board a steamship, since Twain preferred that type of conveyance over the stagecoach, partly out of nostalgia for his Mississippi days, but primarily because boats had saloon facilities and stages did not. (This was long before the days of bar cars on trains, and somewhat before there were *any* trains running between San Francisco and other points on the Pacific Coast besides Nevada.)

In Sacramento, Twain and his business manager dreamed up a sensation-laden publicity campaign. Posters announcing Twain's Sandwich Islands lecture advised potential hearers that Twain would dispense his wisdom from the lecture platform for one night only. . . and for only a portion of that night. The advertising went on:

THE CELEBRATED BEARDED WOMAN! (Is not with the Circus.) THE WONDERFUL COW WITH SIX LEGS! (Is not attached to this Menagerie.) That Curious and Unaccountable Freak of Nature, THE IRISH GIANT! Who stands 9 feet 6 inches in height and has a breadth of beam in proportion . . . will not be present and need not be expected. THE KING OF THE ISLANDS! failed to arrive in season for the Lecture in San Francisco, but may confidently be expected on this Occasion.

As before, the wisdom was scheduled to flow at eight.

The Sacramento event went off as well as had the one in San Francisco, with a capacity house and favorable notices in the Sacramento *Union* and *Bee*. After the lecture was over, Twain paid a visit to his friends Anthony and Morrill at the *Union*, this time trying to convince them to send him on an all-expenses-paid trip around the world in exchange for a further series of travel letters. However, Anthony and Morrill kept their purse strings closed this time, pre-

---

ferring to see Twain pursue his lecturing career and their own solvency maintained a while longer.

Leaving the "City of Saloons," Twain and McCarthy commenced on an itinerary of mining towns that included, in California, Marysville, Grass Valley, Nevada City, Red Dog, and You Bet; and in Nevada, Virginia City, Carson City, and Gold Hill. In Grass Valley, Twain and McCarthy were approached by a former compositor on the *Enterprise* whose wife had a tightrope-walking act. She was scheduled to stage a performance in Grass Valley on the same night that Twain had planned to lecture there. Her husband suggested that Twain combine his lecturing performance with that of the tightrope walker, after a fashion—he proposed that his wife do her tightrope walking outside the hall where Twain was to speak, since the crowd that she drew would then have a tendency to drift into the auditorium to hear Twain's lecture. McCarthy and Twain demurred, seeing the inherent flaw in this reasoning almost immediately.

Also in Grass Valley, Twain carried his flamboyant advertising one step further. In the poster advertising his lecture, he declared that after the lecture was over he would perform a series of "wonderful feats of SLEIGHT OF HAND, if desired to do so." At a given signal, he promised, he would go out with any gentleman member of the audience and take a drink. Also, if the public wished, he would repeat this "unique and interesting feat" until the audience was firmly convinced that this was no act of bogus legerdemain. Furthermore, the poster declared, Twain would, at a moment's warning, leave town without paying his hotel bill. He claimed that he had previously performed this trick on many other occasions, both in San Francisco and elsewhere, and that it had always been received with enthusiastic comment—although he neglected to say from whom these comments issued. Finally, he advertised, "at any hour of the night, after 10," he would "go through any house in the city, no matter how dark it may be, and take an inventory of its contents, and not miss as many of the articles as the owner will in the morning."

DURING HIS FIRST LECTURE

tour, Twain found himself speaking before well-heeled patrician listeners in opera houses with red-velvet drop curtains and bright footlights, and he also dispensed his Sandwich Islands wisdom to audiences of rusty miners in mining camp "academies" with only a row of smoking tallow candles or kerosene lanterns to separate him from his listeners. Wherever he spoke, he always came onstage carrying his lecture notes under his arm. These notes had been printed on brown wrapping paper in very large letters (Clemens's handwriting was unusually large anyway) so that he could make them out under various adverse lighting conditions. The sheets of wrapping paper were generally out of order, and Twain got a good deal of mileage out of shuffling them flamboyantly until they finally attained some semblance of continuity.

One of Denis McCarthy's most important functions as tour manager was to secure, in each town, a person to introduce the speaker. This convention was widespread in the lecture-crazy days of the mid-nineteenth century, and it would have been unthinkable for Twain not to have someone introduce him before he began to speak. Later, he would assume this office himself, stating that he was as capable as anyone else of enumerating his own virtues, but during his first lecture tour he did not attempt to break with tradition. The last-minute scramble for an introducer led to many totally unforeseen introductions. In Red Dog, a tiny mining town on the Stanislaus River, an introducer had been selected prior to the lecture, but he failed to show up at the appointed time. McCarthy was obliged to scan the audience desperately for a last-minute proxy, suitable or otherwise. Finally he plucked an old miner out of the assemblage – a very reluctant old fellow who tried to slip out of McCarthy's iron grip, but failed. He was half-dragged, half-carried to the platform, where he cleared his throat, glanced around wildly, and said, "Ladies and gentlemen, this is the celebrated Mark Twain from the celebrated city of San Francisco, with his celebrated lecture about the celebrated Sandwich Islands." Twain rarely had an introduction as ludicrous as that one, unless you counted the time in another California mining town when a grizzled old sourdough was dragged up to the podium. This savage grumbled, "Ladies and gentlemen, I know only two things about this man; the first is that he's never been in jail, and the second is I don't know why."

As HIS LECTURING CAREER

went on, Twain would develop his platform manner, gradually refining the somewhat unsavory persona that had met with such success in mining camps in California and Nevada but would have horrified staid Eastern audiences who thought Charles Dickens was racy. Twain would also attenuate the drawl that caused one member of a California mining town audience to inquire, after a lecture, "Be them your natural tones of eloquence?" But in 1866, as he was launching his lecturing career, Twain knew that his Pacific Coast audiences loved nothing better than off-color stories interspersed with hard information. Speaking before these audiences, he was more able to express himself in a natural, conversational manner, and his flights of descriptive fantasy were less hampered by the require- ments of convention. Ultimately, his speech-influenced style of writ- ing and lecturing would do much to liberate American literature from the almost terminal politesse that was threatening to choke it to death during the nineteenth century; and the fresh air of Califor- nia was an ideal atmosphere in which that style could grow to maturity.

After finishing up the last of his California lecturing engage- ments, Twain turned next to Nevada—not without a sense of fore- boding, since he had left Virginia City in the spring of 1864 with "his face black before the people of Washoe," as the Gold Hill *Evening News* had sneered at the time. Now Twain wondered whether the specter of the Sanitary Fund fiasco was still hanging ominously over his head—but, as it turned out, that dark cloud had blown away in the years he had been in San Francisco. In Virginia City Twain was received with joy by Joe Goodman, Steve Gillis, and the others on the *Enterprise*, and his lecture there was attended by a large and "most fashionable" audience, many of whom seemed glad that the prodigal Twain had returned to lecture in his old haunts. As might have been expected, the *Enterprise* gave Twain plenty of publicity, both in advance of the lecture and after it was over. Twain was so thrilled with his reception in Virginia City that he wrote happily to his mother and sister in Hannibal that "even though the flush times are past, and it has long been impossible to more than half fill the theatre here . . . they filled it for me, night before last—full—dollar all over the house."

But it was only after lecturing in Carson City that Twain felt absolved of his Sanitary Fund trespasses. He had never been one of that city's favorite people, even before he had given its fair ladies hell in the pages of the *Enterprise*, but his lecture there was nevertheless

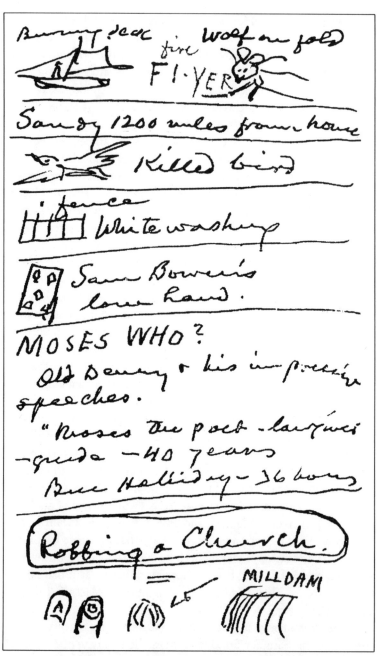

TWAIN'S LECTURE NOTES WERE HIGHLY IDIOSYNCRATIC,
AS IS EVIDENCED BY THESE EXAMPLES FROM AN EARLY LECTURE.

well attended, with Carson's best citizens assembling to hear Twain, in his own words, "disgorge as much truth as I can pump out without damaging my constitution." All in all, it was a triumphant return to Washoe, and Twain was glad that his years in California, along with his growing literary reputation, had made him more acceptable to the Nevadans.

His original lecture itinerary had included several more towns in Washoe, but shortly after his triumphs in Virginia City and Carson City, Twain experienced something that caused him to cancel the remainder of his lectures and hasten back to San Francisco. As he and Denis McCarthy were walking back to Virginia City after Twain had lectured in Gold Hill, they were set upon by a band of highway robbers and presented with that age-old dilemma: "Your money or your life!"

The two forked over their money and some other valuables, including a gold watch that Twain had been given by members of Virginia City's local government during his days on the *Enterprise*, and which was one of his most prized possessions. The highwaymen then fled, leaving a very shaken Twain to wonder how it had happened.

The next day, he found out precisely how it had happened, for it turned out that the irrepressible Steve Gillis and other wags from the *Enterprise* had been behind the "holdup," and it had been nothing but a colossal practical joke, or perhaps Gillis's idea of welcoming Twain back to Washoe. The moment Twain heard this, his mood changed rapidly from shaken and depressed to furious. As we have seen, he could never appreciate a joke if he happened to be the butt of it, and as far as he was concerned, this was the worst joke anyone had ever played on him. It is possible that his anger stemmed from his belief that he had shown too much fear and trembling during the "holdup," and his shame at possibly having disgraced himself in front of his friends, who had posed as the highwaymen. But when he discovered that Denis McCarthy had been in on the plot, Twain's anger knew no bounds, and he paid McCarthy off immediately and informed him with considerable heat that he had no further need of his services. Then Twain returned to San Francisco, abruptly cutting short his lecture tour. He had originally intended to speak again in Virginia City the night after the "holdup," but his confidence had fled, and with it, for the time being, his whole interest in lecturing.

A PREDICAMENT.

After a brief respite,

Twain was forced by financial necessity to take to the public platform and put together a new lecture, once again using the Sandwich Islands as his topic. He promised his public that the new lecture would conclude with "the only true and reliable history of the late revolting highway robbery perpetrated upon the lecturer at dead of night." News stories about the "holdup" had been appearing in San Francisco and Washoe papers, and there were some cynical folks who suspected that Twain had actually staged the whole business himself in order to pump up publicity for his lectures. A writer calling himself "Sans Souci," writing in the *Golden Era*, observed that whiskey cost two bits per glass on board a steamship, and further insinuated that if Twain wanted to gather together enough money to travel, as he was always threatening to do, then he needed to pack in good-sized audiences.

The size of the audience attending Twain's second San Francisco lecture at Platt's Hall on November 16, 1866, was enormous. If anything, this was an even larger group than the one that had crammed into Maguire's Opera House a month earlier. They gathered to hear a lecture that Twain had billed, somewhat tongue-in-cheek, as a "Farewell Benefit"—for he was indeed thinking of traveling again, with New York as one possible destination, and his old home state, Missouri, as another. It had been nearly six years since Clemens had seen his mother, sister, and childhood friends in Hannibal, and he was feeling understandably homesick. However, his plans were not final yet, and at that point the "Farewell Benefit" was more of a humorous reference to his eternal restlessness than it was to any concrete intentions on his part.

The second lecture unfortunately turned out to be something of a failure; at any rate it was not an unqualified success, as its predecessor had been. The San Francisco papers were fairly uniform in their criticism of it, complaining that Twain had padded it out too much with dirty and tasteless jokes. Some of these, the critics felt, were so improper that the female members of the audience hadn't been able to laugh at them without compromising themselves. Worse, at least in the eyes of San Francisco's arbiters of taste, the new lecture had shirked education, choosing instead to embrace mere entertainment. The papers also hinted darkly that Twain's ardent supporters—of which there were admittedly many—had expected better of him than such tactics, and that Twain would be wise not to disappoint them again.

Despite this outpouring of negative opinion, Twain proceeded to lay out another lecturing itinerary that would take him to the surrounding cities of "San Jose, Petaluma, and Oakland, with a final lecture in San Francisco to cap them off." About this time, however, the Washoe *Evening Slope* carried a small news item in its pages that claimed that the proceeds of Twain's ill-starred "Benefit" lecture had been attached by one of his creditors, probably to pay for hotel rooms or other incidental expenses in Virginia City or Carson City. Evidently Twain's promise to leave town without paying his hotel bill had been genuine—either that, or maybe Denis McCarthy had not been keeping honest books. This may have been the reason why Twain scheduled this extra group of lectures without preparing any new material, for by this time his Sandwich Islands repertory was getting fairly worn around the edges.

In San Jose, he employed a tactic that would hardly have been out of place in the sideshow of a two-bit carnival; he offered, from the platform, to demonstrate cannibalism "as practiced in the Sandwich Islands." However, he told his astonished audience, he needed a volunteer. If any mother in the audience would be good enough to bring her child up to the platform, he would commence with the demonstration. Then he waited, with a perfectly straight face, as if he expected a volunteer to step forward any minute. This gambit was so successful at eliciting belly laughs from a large portion of his audience that he often used it in the lectures that followed.

In Oakland, misfortune dogged Twain's lecture at College Hall. There was a misprint on the handbill announcing the lecture, for one thing, which led to a very scanty turnout; the printer had apparently gotten the time of the lecture wrong by several hours. Worse, Twain was kept standing in the wings of the auditorium while a school band ran through what seemed to be an interminable repertory of songs. Twain was perhaps beginning to comprehend Prentice Mulford's earlier admonitions about the difficulties faced by a traveling lecturer.

But things looked up when, in San Francisco, Twain received a letter written by twenty prominent citizens, asking him to repeat his original Sandwich Islands lecture, which some of them claimed not to have heard. (They tactfully left out any mention of the second lecture.) Twain responded with a hearty letter, naming the date for the new lecture—December 10. Announcements in the San Francisco papers described the features of this lecture, which, as before, included "a description of the great volcano Kilauea and the extinct volcano of Haleakala, a mention of Bishops Staley and Harris, and a description of the peculiarities of the Islanders," with the further addition of "many uncommonly bad jokes." (This last was probably a dig at the critic who had sneered at his off-color humor.) Finally, announced Twain, since this was positively his last farewell benefit, he would close with a farewell speech composed for the occasion.

By now Twain's travel plans were clear. He had contracted with the *Alta California* to serve as their traveling correspondent, and he intended to make a circuit of the globe, perhaps stopping in China to visit Anson Burlingame; but first he would visit his family in Hannibal, and he also wanted to see New York again. He further dreamed of attending the gala Paris Exhibition, but his plans were subject to change and modification. Once again, Twain was more interested in the idea of traveling than he was in the reality. He did

CONGRESS HALL

BUSH STREET, JUST ABOVE MONTGOMERY

ON MONDAY EVENING DEC. 10, 1866

MARK TWAIN

will deliver a

LECTURE ON THE SANDWICH ISLANDS
(GRASS SHACKS OF HAWAII)

Chewing on sandwich island
before a good paying audience
has fed me.

WHEREIN DESCRIPTIVE MENTION will be made of the Great Volcano of Kileaua and the extinct volcano of Haleakala.

Much entertaining information will be furnished, and many uncommonly bad jokes indulged in. The performance to conclude with an IMPROMPTU FAREWELL ADDRESS, gotten up last week, especially for the occasion.

THIS is positively the last "farewell benefit" of the lecturer, who sails for the East in the Opposition Steamer on the 15th of the present month.

The Box office will be open all day Monday. No extra charge for reserved seats.

A SPLENDID ORCHESTRA
is in town, but has not been engaged.

Admission ..... One Dollar

A POSTER FOR TWAIN'S LAST
LECTURE IN SAN FRANCISCO; NOTE THE REFERENCE
TO THE "IMPROMPTU FAREWELL ADDRESS,
GOTTEN UP LAST WEEK."

seem to have some intention of returning to San Francisco whenever his wanderings chanced to cease; nonetheless his "farewell speech" seemed to carry more than a little hint of finality, as if he knew his time in California was drawing to a close.

His farewell lecture was received warmly by all in attendance, even the overblown and conventional apostrophe attached to its posterior, in which Twain waxed uncharacteristically verbose about all the wondrous developments that he knew in his heart of hearts would take place in the city by the Golden Gate. His fans knew, when he left the stage for the last time, that their adopted son was taking his Pacific Coast reputation and heading for greener pastures, but they had no way of knowing just how high his star would rise during the next few years. Perhaps some of them truly would miss him; others were probably glad to see him go; but no one who had known anything of Mark Twain in San Francisco had gone untouched by his peculiar genius.

And so we come to the

end of this yarn. On December 15, 1866, Samuel Clemens boarded the steamship *America* and headed out of San Francisco Bay for the last time, en route to New York. He would never see California again for any length of time, although he would spend three months in San Francisco in 1868, rewriting travel material originally published by the *Alta California* for his book, *The Innocents Abroad*, which was to establish him as an important American author with a lasting reputation.

What did California mean to Twain? His feelings about the place were always highly ambivalent. On the one hand, he could refer to California and San Francisco as "the friendliest land and liveliest, heartiest community on our continent," and honestly mean it; and he could also, with equal intensity, curse San Francisco as lawless, ugly, and backward, or complain about the shabbiness that lurked just beneath its gaudy veneer.

However, even Albert Bigelow Paine, who generally gave California little credit for Twain's development as a writer, was able

[Following two pages]
Before bidding farewell to California forever in 1868, Twain had this "menu" for a bogus banquet printed up in San Francisco for circulation among his friends.

LICK HOUSE

STATE BANQUET

GIVEN BY

Messrs. Clemens and Pierson,

(At the expense of the Proprietors of the Hotel,)

TO THEIR

Customary Dinner Companions.

The seats will remain in their usual order or arrangement, thus:

	Mrs. Coghill.	Mr. Ensign.	Mrs. Sherwood.	
Mr. Coghill.				Capt. Osgood.
	Mr. Latham.	Mr. Clemens.	Mr. Pierson.	

Dinner begins at 6 P. M.

San Francisco, Saturday, May 16th, 1868.

BANQUET.

Soup.

Ku-Klux-Klan.   Soupçon de soupe.

Fish.

Whale, Esquimaux style.   Tadpoles.

Angle Worms.

Cold.

Ham, *also*, Shem and Japhet.

Devilled Crabs.   Devilish Lobsters,
Corned Beef.   Corned Boarders,
                        Coffee.

Boiled.

Job (*obscure, but Scriptural*),   Owl.

Entrees.

Grand Entrée from the Circus.
Terrapin, Seraphim, Cherubim and sich.
Grass Widows a la Sherwood.
Veal Pie (made out of horse, there being no veal in market.)
Broiled Missionary, with mushrooms, a la Fi-ji islands
Beefsteak, Goodyear's patent.
Veuve Fell, " twin " sauce.
Double Eagles on toast.

Roast.

Invited Guest, stuffed.
Shoulder of Mountain, mint sauce.
Buzzard.
Saddle of Mutton, with bridle and other harness.

Relishes.

Horse Radish. (If a radish horse is not agreeable, a greenish one will be
provided.)
Pain Killer.   Castor Oil.
            Mexican Mustang Liniment,   S. T. 1860 X.
Spaulding's Prepared Glue.   Benzine.

Vegetables.

Green corns, bunions, etc.   Brickbats.   Mucilage.
Poison Oak.   Sherry Blossoms.

Pastry.

Humble Pie.   Pie Ute.
Duff.   Doughnuts.
Grasshoppers, Digger style.   Oil Cake.
Nut-crackers, Screw-drivers, Anvils.

Dessert.

Forty Mile.   Great Sahara.
Nicholson Pavement Oases.
Ice Cream and Onions.   Strawberries and Garlic.

---

to admit that California had contributed materially to Twain's genius during his two-and-a-half-year sojourn in the state. "He had come away, in his early manhood, a printer and a pilot, unknown outside of his class," said Paine. "He was returning a man of thirty-one, with a fund of hard experience, three added professions — mining, journalism, and lecturing — also with a new name, already famous on the sunset slopes of its adoption, and beginning to be heard over the hills and far away. In some degree, at least, he resembled the prince of a fairy tale who, starting out humble and unnoticed, wins his way through a hundred adventures and returns with gifts and honors."

What effect did those "hundred adventures" that Twain experienced in California subsequently have on him, and on his future as America's greatest author? Twain's California experiences always lay close to his heart, whether he remembered them with love, or, as on occasion, with loathing.

Probably the most poignant demonstration of what his foot-loose California days had meant to him came in Twain's later days, when an old California friend wrote to him in New England, asking him to return to California for old times' sake.

Twain answered in an unreservedly emotional manner. "Those were the good old days, the old ones!" he exclaimed. "They will come no more. Youth will come no more. They were so full to the brim with the wine of life; there have been no others like them.

"Would you like to have me come out there and cry?"

SELECTED BIBLIOGRAPHY

GENERAL

Benson, Ivan. *Mark Twain's Western Years*. Palo Alto: Stanford University Press, 1938.

Branch, Edgar M., ed. *Clemens of the Call*. Berkeley: University of California Press, 1969.

Clemens, Cyril. *Young Sam Clemens*. Portland, Maine: Leon Tebbetts Editions, 1942.

Fatout, Paul. *Mark Twain on the Lecture Circuit*. Bloomington: Indiana University Press, 1960.

Gillis, William R. "Memories of Mark Twain and Steve Gillis." *The Banner*, Sonora, California, (1924).

Kaplan, Justin. *Mark Twain and His World*. New York: Simon and Schuster, 1974.

Paine, Albert B. *Mark Twain, A Biography*. Vol. 1. New York: Harper and Bros., 1912.

Smith, Henry Nash, and Anderson, Frederick, eds. *Mark Twain: San Francisco Virginia City Territorial Enterprise Correspondent*. San Francisco: Book Club of California, 1957.

Smith, Henry Nash, and Anderson, Frederick, eds. *Mark Twain of the Enterprise*. Berkeley: University of California Press, 1957.

Taper, Bernard, ed. *Mark Twain's San Francisco*. New York: McGraw-Hill, 1963.

Walker, Franklin. *San Francisco's Literary Frontier*. Berkeley: University of California Press, 1950.

Walker, Franklin, ed. *The Washoe Giant in San Francisco*. San Francisco: George Fields, 1938.

BOOKS BY MARK TWAIN

Clemens, Samuel. *Roughing It*. New York: Harper and Row, 1913.

Clemens, Samuel. *The Autobiography of Mark Twain*. Edited by Charles Neider. New York: Harper and Row, 1966.

Clemens, Samuel. *Mark Twain's Notebooks and Journals*. Vol. 1, 1855–1873. Berkeley: University of California Press, 1975.

Clemens, Samuel. *Mark Twain's Satires and Burlesques*. Berkeley: University of California Press, 1967.

MISCELLANEOUS MATERIALS

Hirst, Robert H. "How Bret Harte Edited 'The Innocents Abroad'." Thesis, University of California, Berkeley.

Goodwin, C.C. "Samuel L. Clemens—Mark Twain." In *As I Remember Them*. Privately published, 1913.

NOTES

In addition to the books mentioned above, I made use of the materials in the Mark Twain Papers at the University of California, Berkeley, and material supplied by John Ahouse of the California State University, Long Beach, library's special collections, as well as material from the Los Angeles public library's main branch and from the special collections of the University of California, Los Angeles. The MTP collection consists largely of letters written by and sent to Mark Twain, newspaper clippings pertaining to his life and work (some of which were in Clemens's own possession), and Twain memorabilia.

A number of the books listed in this bibliography have, unfortunately, gone out of print, most notably Franklin Walker's valuable survey of the San Francisco literary scene during the mid-nineteenth century, *San Francisco's Literary Frontier*. Others were published by university presses or in limited editions and may not be easy to find.

SUGGESTED READING ON MARK TWAIN

For an overview of Twain's philosophy and his ultimate influence on American thought, I recommend Maxwell Geismar's *Mark Twain: American Prophet* (Boston: Houghton-Mifflin, 1970). Lucius Beebe's *Comstock Commotion* (Palo Alto: Stanford University Press, 1954) gives a colorful, if not strictly factual, history of the Virginia City *Territorial Enterprise* and sheds some light on Twain's early experiences as a journalist.

The best writer on Twain, however, remains Twain himself. As Robert Hirst, editor of the Mark Twain Papers, pointed out to me, "Twain's legend is just as important as the facts about him are." Best of all, Twain's various books are still readily available in libraries and many bookstores; the nineteenth-century author refuses to die.

INDEX